Ambassadors and Zombies

Published by Green Publications

Copyright © 2018 Adam Tangent

Adam Tangent has asserted his right
under the Copyright, Designs and Patents Act 1988
to be identified as the author of this work.

ISBN 978-1-71741-418-2

Also available as a Kindle ebook
ISBN 978-1-84396-516-9

A catalogue record for
this book is available from the British Library
and the American Library of Congress

Cover design and artwork
Paul Morris
www.mostlygreenstuff.com

Pre-press production
eBook Versions
27 Old Gloucester Street
London WC1N 3AX
www.ebookversions.com

*For Lady Brenda and
Mrs Beaver in the school office*

Ambassadors and Zombies

A Teacher's Guide to Schools and Teaching

Adam Tangent

GREEN PUBLICATIONS

Contents

A

Assemblies

Ambassadors

Abbreviations and Acronyms

The school day always used to begin with an **assembly**. Now, however, it is often shunted to the end of the school day so that *learning* can begin the minute pupils get to school. It wasn't very long ago that Senior Management were grateful to anyone willing to do an assembly. There didn't seem to be any programme but there was room for a bit of individuality and eccentricity. The Head of RE in my old school, rather unwisely, did an assembly on 'beavers' to the upper years, which prompted a few raised eyebrows from the staff standing at the side of the hall, and one particularly dull Deputy Head was feted with ironic applause at intervals during his assembly on 'different kinds of holes'. When I started teaching the old Headmaster swept up to the lectern in his academic gown, opened the bible at what seemed to be random pages, and read a short lesson, whilst the first Deputy leaned on the grand piano staring out menacingly at the rows of boys, daring them to misbehave.

Now only members of the Senior Leadership Team (SLT) are entrusted with the long list of worthy assembly topics: Recognition of Achievement, Anti-bullying Week, Equality and Diversity, Determination and Perseverance, Global Enterprise

Week, Universal Children's Day, etc. All of this comes with a daunting list of *Key Terms* (Engagement, Concentration, Determination, Resilience, Confidence, Focus, Positivity, etc.) and a snippet of text (*Pause for Thought*) from various weighty figures – Gandhi, Buddha, Shakespeare, the Dalai Lama and Barack Obama.

The American basketball player Michael Jordan and his quote '*make it happen*' is also very much standard assembly fare at the moment. Members of SLT are fond of quoting Team Sky's cycling teams' maxim *marginal gains* as they attempt to cajole Year 11 (the fifth year) into working harder and taking the year more seriously, but might need to look for a new inspirational role model after all the bad publicity and reports of drug use. Year 11 are always being exhorted to work harder in order to achieve their (or rather the school's) Target Grades and file out of the hall with phrases like 'a ready to learn attitude' and 'tools to succeed' ringing in their ears. Whatever the time of year revision should already have started – cue graphic of a calendar / clock showing the number of days and hours to go until the exams start.

Occasionally assemblies will reflect events and issues in the outside world. To coincide with National Egg week one member of staff opened their assembly by announcing 'I like eggs' before asking the massed ranks of pupils if they liked eggs. When the various opinions on eggs were shouted out order quickly broke down and the teacher went berserk. The whole year group were detained at the end of the day on Friday for a re-run of the assembly.

The annual Remembrance Assembly tends to bring out the best in pupils and despite being crammed in on the floor like sardines they invariably behave impeccably. They also observe the two-minute silence at eleven o'clock, even though it comes in the middle of morning break and the playground will suddenly fall still and silent. The regular old boys who used to attend the assembly and sit up on the stage have fallen away. Instead the reading has been done recently by a relatively young Old Boy. In his first year at the school he came to be known affectionately as the 'buffoon' and far from possessing any military pedigree, he always fainted whenever I showed his class a video which contained any violence or bloodshed. When John Malkovich's Lennie crushes Curley's hand in *Of Mice and Men*, the boy fell off his chair and slid under the table. A few moments later another boy put up his hand and said, 'Sir, Alfie's gone again. Shall I fetch Mrs Patterson?' Hard not to think about that as he gravely intones the 'We shall remember them' over the rows of bowed heads.

Sometimes there's an outside speaker or act. Last year a rap singer came to talk to Year 9 as part of his 2017 School Tour. As well as performing three of his own songs, he promised a 'little conversation on cyber bullying and four core British values'. It wasn't allowed to resemble a traditional school assembly and when he wasn't singing or dancing the artist sat on the edge of the stage hunched over his microphone. He began with, 'What's up, guys?' The pupils quickly caught on that, because of the microphone, he and they could talk simultaneously and he could still be heard. When the noise level / shouting out threatened to get out of hand he asked them to 'chill it'. The problem with having a 'little conversation' is that some of the boys, particularly, say stupid things, either deliberately or unwittingly, and the chorus of derision which followed undermined his message of mutual respect.

Assemblies seem to be on the wane. They've certainly become much less frequent, which isn't surprising as nobody particularly seems to enjoy them. Even my daughter, who is at primary school, comes home groaning about the latest motivational song or slogan. What used to be called a 'daily act of worship' has become a 'moment for quiet reflection', which doesn't tend to be high on pupils' list of priorities. The physical discomfort involved in sitting on the floor also seems to have become a bigger issue in recent years. Just as undergraduates applying to university halls of residence now insist on en-suite bathroom facilities, pupils have the nerve to ask for the chairs to be put out. Making pupils sit cross-legged on the floor is one way of controlling them and probably works better than having them in chairs, unless somebody breaks wind, and then the reaction of other pupils tends to be more exaggerated and harder for the teacher giving the assembly to ignore. The only option is to pretend you haven't noticed and press on.

Abbreviations and acronyms, on the other hand, and also **acrostic** slogans, are on the march in schools. They're everywhere.

At my secondary school, which I attended in the late 1970s and early 1980s, there were PE teachers (Physical Education), RE teachers (Religious Education), and also a TD teacher (Technical Drawing). They were the only abbreviations I can recall and seemed to be reserved for the subjects no one took very seriously – perhaps a mark of their diminished status.

TD was a hangover from when the school had been a Technical School – when it had simply been known locally as the Tech. The teacher was an enormously fat man called Bill Surly and was a law unto himself. For some reason we all knew and were encouraged (by him) to use his first name. Bill was a genial figure in the confines of his classroom, with his shopping bag and thermos flask, but was liable to physically assault you if he saw you doing something he didn't like in the corridor. However, if you chose to study TD for O Level, the rumour was that he looked after you when it came to the final exam – the curtains at the back of the room would be drawn, along with the answers on the blackboard.

TD has now disappeared from schools but has been replaced by a dizzying array of new letters. In one meeting I attended last year SLT (the Senior Leadership Team) and HODs (Heads of Department) discussed the following agenda items: CATs (Cognitive Abilities Tests), PP (Pupil Premium), a 'really powerful data analysis tool' called SISRA (Service for Improved Schools' Results Analysis) which is supposed to help us track EAP (pupils' Expected Attainment Pathway), and I expect T&L (Teaching and Learning) was also mentioned at some point. Last year some schools were also introduced to VESPA – a programme for sixth formers which stands for Vision, Effort, Systems, Practice and Attitude, and which invariably appears next to a picture of a scooter. There's also something called DTF, which is a new T&L initiative called Drive to Fly. Not long after the DTF meetings had commenced and **ambassadors** and **champions** had been established, it was discovered that the letters were also listed on the online dictionary of slang as standing for something else rather rude. (There isn't any obvious difference between **ambassadors** and **champions**. They are usually called Departmental Ambassadors / Champions and are teachers who have volunteered to attend extra meetings or do some more work whilst pretending to be excited about it.)

I also had to attend a RAP meeting – not a forum for teachers to *freestyle* and *dis* their colleagues, but another opportunity for a conversation about Raising Academic Progress. The current obsession with having everything colour coded in red, amber and green has also given teachers RAG sheets.

Like the 'toad *work*' in Philip Larkin's poem *Toads*, abbreviations have also come to 'squat on my life' as an English teacher, apparently in order to make the whole business more professional. First there was the NLS (National Literacy Strategy) and the imposition of re-writing all lesson plans to cater for its tri focus of *Word Level, Sentence Level* and *Text Level*, and then came the dreaded APP and the bewildering Assessing Pupil Progress grids which we were supposed to cross reference every time we marked a piece of work. And now all secondary school pupils know that everything in their English lessons generally boils down to PEE – Point, Evidence, Explain – so that some of them find it impossible to write anything unless they can use a *PEE chain*. My son came home from school last week very grumpy with his English teacher for accusing him of 'violating' a 'PEE chain'.

A good illustration of current teaching orthodoxy was a lesson I observed which was taught by one of the candidates for a vacant Assistant Head Teacher position – the one with responsibility for T&L. The power point slides were full of controlling messages, just in case any of the pupils ventured off task / message – rather unlikely given that the Head and Deputy Head were popping in and out. One corner of the white board was taken up with the acronym PAUSE, which stood for Punctuality, Attitude, Uniform, Sit and Engage. In the opposite corner was the ubiquitous Aim High, Work Hard and Be Kind, and there was also a clock feature telling the class how long they had for each task. Built into every activity were aspirational targets (colour coded of course) and something called DIRT (Designated Improvement and Reflection Time) – a variation on TRIP (Time for Reflection and Improvement) – and an extension task called EBI (Even Better If), which my children had moaned about at their primary school.

B

Back to School

Baffed

Brighton Rock

Back to School signs and displays of stationery and school equipment seem to appear in WHSmith and supermarkets before the long summer holiday has even begun, as if the commercial world can't bear the idea of some people being on holiday for six weeks. Their insensitivity is something I've grown used to over the years, along with the cold looks you get when you make too much noise in the pub on the last day of term. In terms of popularity teachers struggle by comparison with other workers in the public sector. Nurses, for example. And firemen. At Christmas the local fire brigade collect money for charity, encouraging shoppers to deposit loose change in their upturned helmets, but it's hard to imagine teachers doing this and getting the same sort of warm reaction.

Baffled, or its shorter form **baffed**, has become the favourite word amongst pupils and some of my colleagues to describe pupils' stubborn and inexplicable imperviousness to understanding simple ideas. This doesn't include genuinely tricky things like quadratic equations or algebra in maths (and in my case long division), or the impenetrable periodic table, or virtually anything from physics, but often shows itself in the form of failing to grasp who is who in a play or film where there are only half a dozen characters.

An Inspector Calls is generally regarded as a straightforward play, actually a bit too obvious for a GCSE exam text, but this hasn't always proved to be the case. Before I could take one group anywhere near the play's themes – the inspector's message of social responsibility and so on – I had a desperate struggle just to establish the various identities of the characters at the start of the play – a family of four, plus one guest.

Pride and Prejudice represents a stiffer challenge in terms of its language but happily the faithful BBC adaptation takes the strain (and fills up about six hours of lesson time) and even some of the most difficult students tend to respond enthusiastically. However, it can be too much for some pupils. One came to see me after their first lesson on *Pride and Prejudice* to tell me he didn't understand it. We'd only read the first chapter (two and a half pages long), watched a bit of the first episode and briefly discussed the rather different view of marriage in 1800.

'What don't you understand?' I asked.

'Just don't understand it, sir.'

Later when we'd got to the end of *Pride and Prejudice* – the TV adaptation not the actual novel – the class had a number of other questions and seemed to take the heated exchange between Elizabeth and Lady Catherine de Bourgh towards the end a bit too much to heart. 'Will Lady Catherine kill Darcy when she finds out about him and Elizabeth?' one boy asked, apparently seriously. This was followed by an even more bizarre question: 'Was Elizabeth drunk when she said yes to Mr Darcy?' So much for the final union being the culmination of their journey away from pride (Darcy) and prejudice (Elizabeth), towards a proper balance of sense and feeling, or sensibility.

This particular class also managed to make a mockery of my *social ladder* activity. What I had thought to be a reasonably water-tight lesson floundered in the face of confusion and apathy. Having been at pains to assure them that there was no wrong answer for this task – positioning the characters in the novel in their place in the social hierarchy – I wasn't prepared to find the Bennet's housemaid Hill positioned two rungs above Mr Bennet, gentleman landowner and her employer.

Last year I read some extracts from *High Fidelity* by Nick Hornby with a particularly difficult Year 10 group, and of course we also watched the film. Despite the cockiness of a few of the boys in the group in relation to girls, I had wondered whether the adult themes – the narrator Rob's acrimonious break-up with his long-term girlfriend Laura, and subsequent review of his other relationships – might be a bit beyond them. In fact the obstacles I encountered were more to do with basic comprehension. At one point in the story the ex-girlfriend phones Rob in tears to tell him that her father has died, and asks him to come to the funeral. Bizarrely, when Laura didn't feature in the next scene at the wake, somehow the idea took hold that it was Laura's funeral. It took a lot of bad tempered arguing to re-establish that Laura was alive, and the class only resumed interest in watching the film when Laura proves her rude health by having sex with Rob in the front of their car.

One of the chief culprits in the Laura death debacle then spent a large part of his next English lesson arguing with another boy about whether you could take a ferry to Mount Everest.

An extract from **Brighton Rock** by Graham Greene, which has been used recently in an AQA specimen GCSE English Language paper, also proved very difficult for one particular class to grasp. My attempt to provide some context and a bit more of the story just made matters worse. Having made a big thing about the title and Pinkie's stick of rock as the murder weapon, the modern film version shows him murdering Hale with a large pebble, and, in the old black and white film, he seems to be pushed from a ghost train. This all just confused the class and prompted a stream of frustrated questions ('So who's that?') and complaints ('I don't get this, Sir...this is moist'). Towards the end of the film the Catholic sub-theme starts to intrude and confused things even further. At one point Rose is seen praying anxiously to a figure of Christ on the cross. Up to this point there had only been little hints of Rose and Pinkie's shared Catholicism so I thought it necessary to stop the film and mention it. As usual I had failed to anticipate what was puzzling them. The only question that came back was an apparently serious enquiry about the figure of Christ: 'Sir, has he got a six pack?'

My own experience at school was that the fog, which smothered my understanding at primary school and at the start of secondary school, started to clear a little in the third year (Year 9). Some pupils remain shrouded in it throughout their time at school, although when you bump into them some years later they have got jobs and seem to be intelligent and perfectly well adjusted. There are also the lucky few, who seem to see everything clearly from the start.

C

Classroom Management

Cover Work

Classroom Management has become the official term for the exhausting business of controlling pupils' behaviour. Officially it's all about ensuring that they're *on task*, but privately it runs much deeper and can cause a teacher to question their ability, their calling and at times their sanity for opting for this profession.

One particularly difficult Year 10 group that I taught announced themselves as such in their very first lesson. Usually even the most disaffected students make a bit of an effort in their first lesson of the year. Something about being given a new exercise book and familiarity not having yet bred contempt for the teacher, tends to ensure a quiet first lesson with any group. Not with this group. I wasn't helped by the hot weather (invariably the return to school in September coincides with three weeks of lovely weather), which made them even more lethargic and my shirt stick to me – not helpful when you are trying to look in control. In fact most of the class were quiet and fairly pleasant but the seven or eight who weren't claimed all of my attention and energy and successfully derailed the lesson.

After three lessons with this group one boy who sat on his own on the back row had yet to complete a single sentence. In our second lesson he split his trousers, which caused a fair amount of disruption, and then interrupted me in full flow to ask if he could 'go to Room 15 to get his packet of biscuits'. Or so I thought. When I challenged him later as to why he hadn't written anything he explained that he didn't have his pencil case – I had refused to let him go and get it from Room 15. Perhaps I am starting to acquire my pupils' habit of turning a deaf ear to everything that is said to them, although the boys in the front row agreed that he had said biscuits.

I very quickly became reliant on the Duty Manager to get through an hour's lesson with this group. The Duty Manager was built like a fridge freezer stack and commanded the pupils' hushed respect when he entered your classroom. The class would immediately stand to attention and the low-level or high-volume conversation would cease the minute he appeared. Having taught him when he was a first year pupil at the school twenty odd years ago I found this rather galling and had probably been a bit condescending towards him in the past. To his credit he didn't hold this against me and was happy to remove any of the really difficult characters when it all got too much.

A quarter of the way into one particularly disastrous lesson with this group I realised I wasn't getting anywhere and walked out of the classroom and continued in the direction of the staff room to consider my options. I had just sent out the most obviously obstructive member of the class, but, with the Duty Manager at home in bed with the flu, I found myself short of fire power. My inability to impose a sensible seating plan had been threatening to punish me and so it proved. The eight or so pupils who worked quietly had all gravitated to the desks along the wall on one side of the room. This left the larger space in the rest of the room as ungovernable bandit territory. This is a bit of an exaggeration. Nobody was fighting, or using bad language or being rude to me personally; it's just that none of the class were paying me or my six lines of text on the board a blind bit of notice.

One of the changes that has resulted from Michael Gove's time as Education Secretary is that this class, in addition to their two English Language papers, will sit final exams on a nineteenth century novel, a Shakespeare play, a twentieth century literary text, a themed unit of poetry and unseen poetry. Perhaps this was in the back of my mind as I downed tools and left the room in despair at my failure to get them to concentrate on six lines.

In the Year Head's office I explained the situation to the boys' Year Manager. He was always unfailingly, almost unfeasibly friendly and helpful – a fantastic advert, it was sometimes whispered in the staff room, for the power of prayer and religious conviction. He accompanied me back to my classroom and the boys immediately went quiet and stood up behind their desks as we entered. Obviously none of this was for my benefit. We delivered a two-part bollocking and while he was there I drove through a new seating plan, and, this time, remembered to make a note of who was sitting where, before the bell went and they piled out for lunch.

The new seating plan put a bit more space between some of the most difficult characters but also encouraged them to call across the room at an even higher volume. Their next lesson was supposed to be on Gerald Croft, the rather bland fiancée in *An Inspector Calls*, but was enlivened by a number of unrelated subplots. Just as I began the introduction one of the boys came in late, brushed past me and furiously squared up to another member of the class, who he accused of writing something about him, or I suspect his girlfriend, on the wall of the boys' toilets. I hurried him out to the Duty Manager and left him to investigate the incendiary toilet text. Back in the classroom another boy announced that he was going home at lunchtime because he was feeling unwell. I encouraged him to go to the Welfare Room where his not working wouldn't disturb the rest of the class, but he was determined to stay and huddled down into the folds of his coat. A girl on the back row then produced a small metal tin of something she claimed was medicinal for the boy's headache and gave it to the most unpredictable member of the class who then set about trying to open it whilst simultaneously complaining about his injured hand / wrist, which was preventing him from doing any work. When he finally got the lid off, the tin seemed to contain pungent axel grease, which he set about applying to the temples of his ailing friend.

This class were more enthusiastic about *Great Expectations* – specifically the new film version – but couldn't help from articulating loudly every single reaction or point of confusion, of which there were many. Old Orlick was referred to as Zombie Man and I found myself having to adopt this for the sake of clarity. Estella elicited mixed reactions. 'She's peng' was the general view of the young Estella amongst the boys in the class, but there was disagreement about the mature character – or rather the actress playing her in the BBC adaptation. And for all their bravado most of the class seemed to be unnerved by Miss Havisham's dry skin and manic hand rubbing.

They managed to watch the final moments of the film in respectful near-silence. The new film delivers a straightforwardly happy ending by engineering a swift reunion between Pip and Estella, whereas the novel makes them wait eleven years. To pad out the lesson I read the last chapter to them and attempted to introduce the concept of pathetic fallacy via some of the rather obvious imagery – Pip's 'mist' clearing with the help of Estella's 'moonlight'. One boy bemoaned the wordiness of these three pages, comparing them unfavourably to *The Diary of a Wimpy Kid*, his preferred reading.

With a particularly difficult group teachers sometimes check the register in the morning, hoping to find certain names marked absent, but relief often turns sour when they turn up to your lesson after coming in late. Inevitably teachers occasionally give in to the temptation of some respite and call in sick themselves. Unfortunately setting **cover work** is sometimes more trouble than going in and muddling through when you are feeling unwell. Subjects like Art and PE have it much easier in this respect. The Head of Art at a previous school used to invent deliberately fatuous cover work for these occasions: 'Design a stick to throw for your pet dog…it must be sticky…Design a bowl for your goldfish…it must contain water…' etc, etc. He was also responsible for running the Fantasy Absence League, for which staff were priced according to their reliability or otherwise. Serious malingerers or ambitious types, constantly out of school to attend training courses, were priced at 50p, whilst honest stalwarts could be picked up for as little as 5p. However insensitive and politically incorrect, it did have the effect of reducing staff absence for the two years it was permitted to run.

There is nothing quite so humiliating as a lesson spiralling disastrously out of control, although officially this isn't supposed to happen. There are strategies and tools to deal with this sort of thing – three warnings (three strikes and you're out), counting down from three or five every time you want the class to be quiet, and drawing smiley and sad faces on the board, under which the teacher writes the names of the good and the bad, not to mention the SIMS behaviour management system – but perversely bad behaviour still persists.

But however badly behaved pupils might be in your lesson, there is always the consolation that they are probably even worse in someone else's class. Teachers aren't above a form of professional schadenfreude, raising their eyes to the ceiling in disapproval when there's an explosion of noise from the class next door or above. On one occasion the explosion was so loud that I left my class and rushed upstairs to investigate what was happening above me, assuming that an unsupervised class were rioting. I arrived at the same time as the Duty Manager to find some of my favourite Year 10 students in uproar, and their Maths teacher standing helplessly behind the door.

Pupils are no respecters of age or experience and seem to have a sixth sense in relation to a teacher's classroom management, and won't hesitate to exploit perceived weakness. Vital intelligence is also passed down from elder siblings about which teachers can or can't be given the run around. One Science teacher at my first school spent years being subjected to rudeness and brazen defiance from pupils who, quite correctly, assumed they could behave with impunity. For some reason he never did anything about it. Another member of the Science Department came across him one day taking a mid-lesson time-out in the chemistry prep room. Through the open door carried the taunts of his waiting class: 'Oi Warren, get back in here and face the music!'

When I was in the third year (Year 9) my Physics class used to fall silent for 'Basher' Mills in about two or three seconds. This probably had a fair bit to do with his fearsome reputation and reports that the slight hollow on the surface of the teacher's desk had succumbed to Basher's bare hands. On one occasion I was the last person to stop talking and Basher cuffed me so hard on the side of my head that I immediately welled up with tears.

D

Data

Discretion

Dreams

Differentiation

Data drops are a relatively new kid on the block in schools and an essential tool for tracking pupils' 'flight path' towards their final destinations and the Holy Grail of *progress*. But progress towards what? Bizarrely the destination (their Target Grade) is fixed at the end of primary school (Year 6) when pupils are eleven, rather like choosing your holiday destination five years before you go. Any number of variables might rear their head between the end of primary school and the end of Year 11 but that doesn't help a school's *progress measure* and so isn't part of the *conversation*. The sort of conversations teachers are encouraged to have with their pupils are along the lines of do they know that 46% of pupils across the country with a similar background will achieve the Target Grade which is currently proving beyond them.

Data drops are demanded with increasing frequency. It's hard not to think of shareholders and executive boards reviewing quarterly sales figures. However futile this might be for teachers and pupils – barring the most unusual circumstances the *Predicted Grades* won't change – it looks good for the Senior

Leadership. When Ofsted come they can show they've been all over the staff like a rash and they will have the data to prove it. One way to calm SLT's fears about the progress of the Year 11s approaching their GCSEs, and to stop them talking about intervention all the time, is to up the Predicted Grades and move pupils out of the red and into orange and green.

Data muscled its way into my teaching life some years ago when the English Department at my old school were unfortunate to be singled out for a mini Ofsted – a subject inspection with a particular, and for us unwelcome focus on the teaching of poetry. The inspector, however, didn't want to talk about poetry, but asked me instead about our *CVA data*. After a sharp intake of breath I had to ask him to explain what it was. It turned out to be *Contextual Value Added* data, and from that moment the whole game seemed to change. There was no longer any way you could say to your Line Manager or the Head Teacher that you thought the results looked pretty good, because they could turn round and say that pupils in schools with similar cohorts were doing much better. Unfortunately there is always a school which breaks ranks and manages to do unfeasibly well, allowing Head Teachers to cite these as examples of *outstanding practice* that we should be looking to emulate.

Discretion is another vital part of the teacher's tool kit. It's not a good idea to gossip to one class about other classes or pupils because their loyalty and discretion cannot be relied upon. Some years ago, when pupils were still required to do course work at home, I had great difficulty in getting a Shakespeare essay out of one particularly difficult pupil. In the end, I rang home and his mother assured me that he was writing it as we spoke and I would have it the next day. I was pleasantly surprised when the boy handed me the essay first thing the following day. As my A Level class were getting settled I glanced at the start of the essay and promptly burst out laughing. The essay he'd given me had nothing to do with the task I had set and appeared to have been stolen from a post-graduate dissertation he'd found on the internet. Foolishly I read out some of the most high-brow passages that the boy was claiming to have written, to my little group of sixth formers. Some sort of honour amongst thieves, however, prompted one of the boys in the class to text the culprit and explain what I was doing with his essay. Before I knew it I had lost the moral high ground and was having to apologise to the boy's parents for ridiculing their son to other boys – parents who had colluded in the bogus course work.

Teaching **dreams** are an occasional and unpleasant side effect of spending the working day in classrooms in the company of school children. They usually involve a disastrous lesson which descends into anarchy. My most recent one placed me in a small American infantry unit involved in a potentially bloody siege. The undisclosed enemy (a year 10 or 11 class?) were coming closer all of the time and I was hugging an enormous machine gun. Fortunately I woke up before the shooting began. I was usually on the receiving end of enemy fire in my first recurrent and troubling teaching dream – a hangover from a teaching practice placement where the lower school pupils had christened me Egon, a character from the film *Ghostbusters*, and regularly took aim at me in the corridor with imaginary slime guns. My chief tormentor – a Year 8 boy called Darren – had introduced this practice in one particularly rowdy English lesson, and continued to open fire on me in my dreams for the next few years.

*　　*　　*

It was probably my fault that Darren and his classmates strayed off task and became preoccupied with 'who they were gonna call' and slime guns. The tutors on the PGCE (Post Graduate Certificate of Education) course would have probably said that it stemmed from my failure to **differentiate** between the different needs of the pupils. One of the other students on the course was taken to task by his tutor after an observed lesson for 'not building bridges to the invisible children'. **Differentiation** (providing different work for pupils with different abilities) remains an important buzz word in education but because it entails extra work and the potentially daunting challenge of having two or three different lessons running simultaneously, isn't a very attractive proposition. It's easier to do in a primary school classroom, where the teacher is a permanent fixture in the classroom and will probably have at least one TA (Teaching Assistant) to help organise different activities on different tables. Much harder for the secondary school teacher who arrives out of breath on the bell. *Learning*, we are constantly reminded, has to begin immediately, so inevitably it's easier to teach one lesson and organise one activity than to differentiate.

There are shortcuts. Differentiation *by outcome* is an attractive option, but probably won't impress an Ofsted inspector. Writing *EBI* (Even Better If) at the end of a pupil's piece of work that you've marked, has now become a common device in secondary teaching to demonstrate *challenge* – that you're *stretching the top end.*

One survival plan / attempt to differentiate that I used with a particularly difficult Year 10 group involved lots of cutting and sticking. Previous attempts to get them to take notes had ended in failure, so I provided everything on a sheet which they had to cut out and arrange in their books. The TA gave me a look, which seemed to say 'I can't see the point of this' / 'This is too babyish', but ended up having to stick one boy's quotes down for him. The subject of the lesson was gender inequality and representation in *An Inspector Calls*. I introduced the topic by showing the class a short film about the death of the suffragette Emily Davison, who ran in front of the King's horse at The Derby in 1913. If I thought that this would have a sobering effect or give some of them pause for thought I was wrong. Freed from the need to think or write, some of the boys in the class kept up a constant stream of eye-wateringly inappropriate conversation about the girls in their social circle. After forty-five minutes one boy had managed to stick one quote into his book. Sensing the teacher's red mist descending I bundled him out of the class and into the Duty Manager's room before I lost it.

Exams

Extra-curricular

Enrichment

It's now all about final **exams**. Pupils like the boy with the plagiarised post-graduate Shakespeare essay, and Michael Gove, have done for course work, which is a shame. If a course work assignment was uninspiring at least you could blame the teacher. Very often pupils responded by producing amazing work. One boy, who went on to become a dentist, dismayed his hard-pressed English teacher by writing twenty seven sides on the computer for his *Pride and Prejudice* essay. Controlled Assessments, on the other hand, which followed course work, were often extremely dull and there was nothing the teacher could do about it. And now English teachers are left with two years at GCSE to practice short reading tasks or the formulaic writing tasks.

It is chastening when marking the Year 10 and 11 GCSE mock exams to see how little of the exam preparation / advice makes it as far as the exam room, and it is tempting to take a sulky vow of silence in the first lesson after the exams to make the point. At least pupils tend to heed the call for creativity and colour on the writing tasks. When urged to employ language devices in their own writing they invariably turn to the simile.

One student, describing getting out of a cramped car after a long journey, 'felt like a brand new foetus leaving the woman'. Less original but equally incongruous was the 'policeman' who 'jumped out of the van like a kangaroo'. More poignant was the description of 'huffing and puffing like a dying panda'.

The English Literature GCSE exam used to be the occasion for the English teacher's annual meltdown / strop – first when pupils were allowed to take their copies of the set texts into the exam, but, apparently oblivious to the advantage, still managed to forget their books; and then more recently, sweating over whether we had enough clean copies and sometimes having to resort to frantically rubbing out their annotations. Not that anyone ever checked. Only once do I recall anyone coming to inspect the school's conduct of public examinations. It was at the very end of the exam season, sometime in the mid-1990s, when teachers still invigilated public exams. The main hall and the sports hall, which were used for the exams, had been returned to their normal use and I was invigilating the final A Level exam in what used to be the Music room. When one of the ladies from the office arrived to warn me of the approaching inspector I was reading *The Daily Mirror*. She suggested I put the paper away and when, a few seconds later, a grave looking man carrying a brief case appeared at the door, I was doing my best to look as if I was taking invigilation very seriously, albeit sitting on a folded up newspaper. I nodded gravely at the inspector as if to say 'everything's under control', and he went away.

After all the work they might have done on texts like *Macbeth* or *Great Expectations* or *Animal Farm*, pupils get a choice of just two questions in the final exam, and the trick is to prepare them for whatever comes up in the exam paper. A few years ago, whilst I was invigilating a GCSE English Literature exam, I challenged a boy in my class, who I had spotted answering on a text that we hadn't read or studied. He replied, 'This one looks easier, sir.'

But sometimes it is the teacher who is at fault. In my first teaching post my Head of Department asked me to teach *Othello* to the A Level English Literature group, not realising that it was no longer on the syllabus. His error went undetected until the boys opened the exam paper and found that there were no questions on *Othello*. The exam was held-up whilst my old Head of Department went off to ring the exam board for further instructions. They very obligingly faxed through alternative questions for *Othello*, allowing him to blame the confusion on a printing error.

The invigilation of public exams has now been outsourced to specialist invigilators – often retired people or housewives – but used to fill large chunks of the Summer Term. In a school exam a teacher can get on with some marking but it wasn't permitted in a public examination. One way of passing the time was to read the graffiti on the old desks. The new desks are blue and slippery and generally unsympathetic to graffiti, but given the filth about other pupils and members of staff etched into the varnished surfaces it's not difficult to see why schools feel the need to invest in new ones. One less offensive line that caught my eye during an invigilation was 'Poetry is gay'.

Another ruse for passing the time was a childish game in which you sent your colleagues off to stand next to the pupil with the silliest haircut or the longest nose.

Even though pupils are encouraged to start their GCSE revision in the Autumn Term in Year 11, Study Leave or Exam Leave has been scrapped in most schools – i.e. the two week period before the exams start, which was previously the moment for intensive revision. The old battle with yourself to keep to the elaborate revision timetable you'd drawn up with a ruler is over for most secondary school pupils. Unless they have an exam many schools insist on them still being in lessons. And once the exams are in full swing this can mean teachers supervising classes of one or two students to whom you have already said all you have to say. This sort of bending over backwards / we must do absolutely everything possible attitude has become the norm and it's hard not to be nostalgic for the way the summer term used to be organised. In my first school pupils were released for Study Leave at the earliest opportunity – sometime at the start of May; and after the May half-term Year 10 exams were stretched out over two weeks and they then disappeared for another three weeks on Work Experience, returning just before the last week of term.

At the other end of the spectrum of what schools do is **extra-curricular**, or, since that has become synonymous with extra-marital affairs, what has become known as **enrichment**. Enrichment began at my old school as the replacement for sixth form General Studies, which the poet Simon Armitage describes, in his poem *You May Turn over and Begin*, as 'a doddle, a cinch for anyone with an ounce of common sense'.

But now enrichment provision covers anything schools offer beyond the classroom. Students are always keen to get out of school by going on trips. One small group of A Level English Literature students studying *Othello* campaigned tirelessly to try to persuade me to take them to Cyprus at half-term – sticking up tourist posters in my classroom, leaving holiday brochures on my desk and even changing my screen saver to a Cypriot beach scene. Sadly for them organising a school trip has become even more onerous in recent years and the trip to Cyprus was never going to happen.

School trips have always been an exhausting business, fraught with difficulties. When I was in the sixth form our English teachers organised a long weekend trip to Stratford-Upon-Avon. There were no seats or seat belts in the school minibus then – we just sat in the back facing each other on the benches along each side of the bus. We had never seen our English teacher drive before, and there were some comments from the back along the lines of 'Where's your bicycle, sir,' his preferred means of transport. Somewhere in the middle of England he approached a roundabout far too quickly and crashed into the back of a black Mercedes with a diplomatic number plate. In fact the mini bus came off worse because, to avoid hitting the Mercedes full-on, he had turned into a raised concrete barrier and badly damaged the suspension. Our group had to sit in a field for three hours waiting to be picked up by a hire bus.

Our teacher had probably never driven the minibus before, a position with which I have some sympathy. In my first teaching job I was asked to take the Year 8 football team to an away fixture at a school about a ten minute drive away. In the event it took me fifteen minutes to get the minibus started, another ten minutes to get it into reverse gear, and another ten to manoeuvre my way out of the school car park. Inevitably one of the many questions to be fired off from the boys in the back was, 'Have you ever driven this before, sir?' but given my alarming level of incompetence, they remained remarkably cheerful and relaxed.

On one trip with GCSE students to the theatre we took the train. Just as our train was approaching one of our boys launched a tremendous kick at another pupil. His slip-on shoe flew across the tracks and over the roof of the platform on the other side. My senior colleague wasn't prepared to tolerate the boy's behaviour or continued presence, and announced that he was taking him back to school, whereupon the boy scarpered to the end of the platform and got on the train which had just pulled in. There was nothing we could do except organise alternative footwear. Somebody leant him a pair of trainers and the matter was forgotten.

One problem with taking groups of teenagers on trips to nice places is that they stick out like a sore thumb and if anything goes wrong, school parties tend to get the blame. When *Captain Corelli's Mandolin* was a bestseller in the 1990s, we organised a Reading Week / Cultural Holiday for the A Level English Literature students to Kefalonia – the Greek island where the novel is set. Most of the trip coincided with half-term and not surprisingly there wasn't a great deal of reading going on. On their third night some of the boys bought spirits in the local mini market, which they consumed out of view on the beach. A drunken game got out of hand and ended up inflicting damage on a couple of sunbeds and a parasol. The next day my colleague and I found ourselves answering questions in the local police station. Suspicion, understandably, had fallen on our group, but the boys swore they knew nothing about it – a position we had to argue to the policeman. With talk of a judge being sent from the mainland to investigate, something had to give, and fortunately two of the boys cracked under the pressure and came clean. George, the taverna owner, whose sunbeds they had damaged, was asking for five hundred pounds, so each of the culprits was made to sign an IOU for seventy-five pounds, to be paid on their first day back at school. When I paid the bill with my credit card, George rang it through the till and gave me a receipt for twelve *Chef Specials*.

My first MFL (Modern Foreign Languages) trip to the Loire Valley involved taking the ferry from Poole across to

Cherbourg. Before it became toxic for teachers to handle cash, the MFL department always travelled with a very generous kitty for staff meals and drinks, and as soon as we were aboard the ferry we sat down to an enormous breakfast. Unfortunately the breakfast only stayed on board me for about half an hour – what should have been a four hour crossing ended up being nearer eight hours of being tossed about on rough seas, throwing up in the toilets, side-by-side with our pupils who were also stricken.

Sadly the kitty and staff staying in hotels, rather than 'families' like the pupils, have become a thing of the past. When I went with the MFL Department to Strasbourg a few years later, the group leader booked himself into a hotel, but the other teachers stayed with host families. My family lived in a rather grand block of apartments. The tiny bedroom I was given had presumably once belonged to one of the servants, and could only be reached up a long stone spiral staircase. Unfortunately the trip coincided with a heatwave and temperatures around 45 degrees centigrade, which meant that each time I returned to my room after taking a shower I was sweating so much that I needed another one.

In Granada, on my last MFL trip, the accommodation was even worse. Four members of staff were put up in a small modern house on the edge of a housing estate still under construction. We shared the house with our Spanish hostess and her extensive collection of soft toys and life-size Lassie dogs.

An encounter with an enormous Alsatian – a real one – is what has remained with me from my own French exchange to Dunkirk in 1983. I woke in the night desperate for the toilet, but acutely aware that the only toilet was downstairs, and could only be reached via the kitchen where the dog had his basket. In the event I only got as far as the living room before the dog pinned me to the wall and barked furiously until the host family came down and rescued me.

These discomforts and indignities – like eating horse meat for dinner - are part of any French or Spanish exchange for the students, and can be put down as character building, but they aren't really what their teachers had in mind when they volunteered for the trip.

F

Fischer Family Trust

Fun

The **Fischer Family Trust** sounds like a make of children's toy or an American cult, but is in fact the provider for a lot of the data used in schools. *FFT D* is a phrase I have often heard from the mouths of Senior Leaders, or *FFT D + 1* – referring to the Target Grades we are being measured against. Strange though it seems to base GCSE targets on what pupils were like in their last year at primary school, you can't even be sure of that target staying the same. Schools can choose to opt for more challenging aspirational targets (*FFT D + 1*, for example) and so condemn teachers and pupils to almost certain failure.

The new FFT computer program has a *dashboard*, which looks like it is supposed to sound – like the controls of a plane, and one of the options teachers can check is called *Turbulence Factors*. There are also things called *Fire Alerts* and *Alert Systems* to help us spot when a student is underperforming – as if we don't know when they do and don't do their homework, or behave in class, or how they have done in their assessment.

Happily it is still possible to have **fun** during lessons. By way of introduction to the Sherlock Holmes story *The Speckled Band*, I organised a mock police identity parade at the start of the lesson. Six volunteers lined up in front of the whiteboard whilst the rest of the class scribbled down Holmes-like deductions based on eagle-eyed observation of their appearance. That was the idea, but as with most *fun* activities which rely on pupil input, the results depend on the class in front of you. This particular class spotted another opening in this activity for insulting each other and came up with deductions like: 'boy 1 looks weak', 'boy 4's head is the shape of a melon', 'boy 2 hasn't washed'. I am not convinced that they really understood the notion of deduction. One boy wrote 'boy 3 is tall'.

When the activity descended into farce I retaliated by making them copy out the text of a correction task, although my original plan had just been for them to circle the mistakes they could find on the sheet. Copying out may be fairly pointless but has a valuable calming effect, and many pupils seem to prefer it to creative thought. 'You can't go to break until it's done,' also has a pleasing absence of ambiguity which pupils respect.

Neither activity would be likely to go down very well in the current educational climate. Not only were the students not learning anything, but even worse, neither activity allowed the teacher to demonstrate progress. Currently it isn't enough for students just to learn, but the process and acquisition of what they've learnt needs to be trumpeted to interested parties or *stakeholders*. This has given rise to an obsession with peer marking (always in green pen) and things like *TRIP* – Time for Reflection and Improvement. And when pupils get their work back it isn't enough now to bask in the warm afterglow of a good mark; they are expected to respond in writing to what their teacher has written – *Yes I promise Miss, I'll try and use more interesting vocabulary in future*, etc. At my daughter's primary school rubbers are banned – the initial mistake and the subsequent learning have to be visible. (If rubbers are out, water bottles are definitely in – an essential part of what primary schools call *brain food*. My daughter's water bottle, she has discovered, has a rubber base which can double as an eraser, and so is much in demand from her friends determined not to besmirch their work with ugly errors.) The pupils are also required to leave a line free after each line of writing for what is called *up-levelling* – basically writing it out again without the mistakes and hopefully a few more *wow words*.

A few years ago the buzz words were very different. Ofsted inspectors, we were told, wanted to see group work and active learning – pupils making posters and putting their ideas down with marker pens on big bits of paper – and learning had to begin the minute pupils entered the classroom. Teachers needed to zip it and let their pupils do the talking, and in the process they would end up learning something. An end to *chalk and talk*. But now it's back, as long as the assessment data tells a story of relentless improvement.

The economic age of austerity seems to have encouraged something similar in school education – an unhealthy fixation with *learning* along Gradgrindian principles. Take, for example, these targets from a Year 11 Aspirations Day: '*In my spare time I will review my work and consolidate information – I will spend twenty minutes per night reviewing work done during the day and learning new facts…*' Or this one under the heading *Study Skills*: '*I will research relaxing bedtime drinks / ways of getting to sleep.*' As if. And what sort of student would want to sign up for this: '*I will ask one question per lesson and then mark the question in my planner.*'

G

Mr Gradgrind

Growth Mind Set

Gifted and Talented

Good

Even **Mr Gradgrind**, the utilitarian educational philanthropist in Dickens' novel *Hard Times*, recognises that there's not much point in subjecting his adopted ward Sissy Jupe to any more schooling:

> 'I fear, Jupe,' said Mr Gradgrind, 'that your continuance at the school any longer, would be useless… You are extremely deficient in your facts. Your acquaintance with figures is very limited. You are altogether backward, and below the mark.'

Now she'd have to stay on at school or go to college and re-take English and Maths, possibly three or four times before she left full-time education at 18. There is an echo of Mr Gradgrind's language in the latest assessment of pupil performance for Key Stage 2 SATs – *working at, or above, or towards the Year 6 standard* ('mark'). This in turn has echoes of the old 11+, which divided pupils up at the end of primary school (KS2). In Kent this was replaced by the Kent Test. School children were informed by post over the summer holiday that they had been classified as either *selected* or *unselected*. For those who were unselected this wasn't a great boost as they got ready to start secondary school, but at least there was a cold logic to this – the division followed them into their new school, either a grammar school or the equivalent of a secondary modern. It's harder to see what purpose these judgements serve now that primary school children nearly all join comprehensive schools, except to help Ofsted rate the school, which is what it's actually about and explains the schools' exhaustive preparation for SATs and the free pre-SATs breakfasts they provide.

In 1978, as I recall, we went into school one day and the teacher had re-arranged the furniture and told us we'd be doing a test in silence. That was it, but it didn't alter anything that was going to happen later – people going on to become doctors, or shop assistants, or lorry drivers, or teachers.

The slogan **Growth Mind Set**, which is currently flavour of the month in primary and secondary schools, puts me in mind of Dickens' description of Mr Gradgrind's bald head – '*its shiny surface, all covered with knobs, like the crust of a plum pie as if the head had scarcely warehouse-room for the hard facts stored inside.*' Schools like malleable all-rounders, who are prepared to work hard across the board, and bring home the bacon / progress measure at the end of Year 11. For *growth mind set*, read willingness to make (warehouse) room for everything their teachers serve up on the long slog to their GCSE exams. What schools don't need are clever pupils, who have high targets, falling way below the expected mark. This can kill a school's progress measure. This means that a number of familiar and not unhealthy scenarios can't be allowed to happen: the pupil puts most of their time and energy into a particular area of interest in which they excel at the expense of other subjects; the pupil has a clear idea of what they want to do after school and decide not to bother with subjects which seem to have no relevance; although the pupil has good powers of understanding, they have no appetite or aptitude for developing their thinking in extended written answers – in short they hate writing; the pupil realises that they will never use any of the mathematics they are struggling with on their GCSE course in their adult life, and gives up the fight.

Primary Schools are particularly keen on pushing the growth mind set. At my daughter's school the correct attitude to *learning* is outlined on a big display entitled *Do I have a growth mindset?* The wrong attitude / way of talking about their school work is corrected with a worthy alternative. *I made a mistake* is replaced by *Mistakes help me learn and improve*, and instead of *I'll never do this, it's too hard*, the right thing to say and think is, *This might just take some time and effort*. There's no room for the sort of educational faint-heartednesss shown by Mr Gradgrind towards Sissy's education, no giving up: *I'm not clever enough to do this* gives way to *I will learn how to do this*.

At the end of *Hard Times*, however, it is Sissy Jupe, '*backward and below the mark*', and who was originally raised in a circus, who has the strength and resilience (another current buzz word in schools) to rescue Mr Gradgrind and his over-manufactured daughter Louisa.

G&T, or **Gifted and Talented**, was one of New Labour's flagship policies – along with Specialist School Status – designed to distance the Blair government from what Alastair Campbell insensitively called the '*bog standard comprehensive*'. It also gave parents the warm feeling of having their child on the G&T *Register*. There must have been a temptation to extend this distinction rather more widely than was really merited, and the lists of pupils identified as G&T certainly raised eyebrows amongst some of their teachers.

In New Labour double-speak G&T was part of the *Strategic Plan* for *inclusion*. The 2005 White Paper entitled *Higher Standards: Better Schools for All*, set out the government's ambition for every pupil (*more able, G&T, struggling or average*) to enjoy the *'right to personalised support'*, although, in truth, there haven't been many initiatives in schools to cater for *average* pupils. The White Paper helpfully conceded that *'the More Able or Gifted and Talented also have the right to leisure'*.

David Cameron's Conservative government weren't ever going to embrace Labour's phrase *Gifted and Talented*, even if the policy is more Conservative than Labour. Ofsted now refer to the *'most able'* or *'highest attainers'*, and a recent report by the Sutton Trust, entitled *Educating the Highly Able,* recommends that the G&T *'construct'* be *'abandoned'*.

At some point in the last few years **good** ceased to be a subjective term and has become a solid, scientifically proven objective entity – as in Ofsted *Good*, or the odious *good practice* (recently overtaken by *best practice*).

Meetings are given over to sharing good practice. Last year the Autumn Term ended with a *Teaching and Learning* Christmas special in the school hall. The plastic dinner tables were covered in festive red paper and covered with offerings from different departments showing *good practice*. Later a member of SLT appeared dressed as Father Christmas and rang a bell. Staff were asked to get into groups of six or seven and sit in a circle. We were joined by one of the *Teaching and Learning Ambassadors* and given a parcel to pass and unwrap every time the (Christmas) music stopped. Beneath each layer was a packet of Haribo in the time honoured fashion of children's parties. The recipient had to earn their prize by sharing details of a lesson that had gone particularly well, or strategies they had used to make learning more effective in their classroom. The Head subsequently described this particular staff meeting as the highlight of his time at the school.

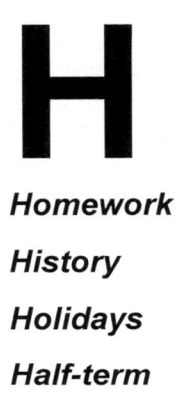

H

Homework

History

Holidays

Half-term

To help teachers with the routine task of setting and collecting **homework** there are now *twenty four hour platforms* like *Real Smart* or *Show My Homework* or *Google Classroom*. On the latest models the homework setting tool now includes *mood data*. Students can tick a box beneath various emojis of happy and sad faces which best reflects their mood from the four categories – *Happy, Frustrated, Struggling* or *Started*. It used to be viewed as a bit of a result if pupils did their homework; now we need them to be happy about it as well. At some point in the future I expect we will be asked to analyse the homework *mood data* for particular cohorts of students. And if they're not in a good mood 'what strategies have you put in place', etc, etc.

My son's mood is never very good when he has Maths homework and I have become used to cooking his tea with a background noise of bitter grumbling, along the lines of 'When am I ever going to need to do this?' It seems to remain the case, for students just starting secondary school, that Maths homework impinges more than any other subject. It helps the teachers that it's easy to set – often the next exercise in the book – and relatively quick and painless to mark. Better still the pupils can mark it themselves using the answers at the back of the text book.

Rather harder work would be organising what educational websites describe as Ofsted *outstanding* homework. This involves *'personalising the children's learning in a safe environment'* – obviously via technology, with something called *learning platforms*. *'Homework platforms'* they suggest *'are an excellent way of meeting Ofsted's recommendations'*. The website then gives an example of good practice – a teacher who used an IRC (Internet Relay Chat) to promote *'new areas of discussion'* and *'facilitate a learning community that would extend the school day in an engaging way'*. Alternatively the teacher could have had the discussion and answered any questions during the lesson, but then they wouldn't have any evidence to show Ofsted.

By means of Bluetooth in the car, I was recently privy to a conversation between my son and one of his classmates about their Biology homework, possibly one of the shortest phone conversations of all time.

My son: 'Reuben, have we got Biology homework?'

Reuben: 'Yeah.'

The end. Chatting about their homework and extending the school day are not high on most pupils' list of priorities.

In Alan Bennet's play *The **History** Boys,* the History teacher Mrs Lintott explains to her new young colleague, Irwin, that one of *'the hardest things for students to learn is that a teacher is human'*. And also that *'one of the hardest things for a teacher to learn is not to try and tell them'*. It is disconcerting to discover early in your teaching career that pupils make little distinction between the trendy young twenty-something teacher (you probably still feel like a real person and not just a teacher) and the grizzled veteran, who is eying up retirement. We are all adults and regarded as impossibly ancient. As a preliminary to studying the play with a group of bright Year 10 students, I asked them to classify different types of teacher they had come across. Several groups listed what they called the *CBs*, which they explained stood for 'conversation beggars' – teachers they perceived as trying to be too matey, almost needy in their dealings with pupils, and guilty of crossing Mrs Lintott's invisible line between teacher and pupil. As well as young teachers the other main culprits were members of Senior Management, prone to making conversation with pupils they pass in the corridor, or at the school gates at the start and end of the day. Greeting the pupils and then seeing them off is a recent Senior Leadership phenomenon, presumably related to good PR and the need to be seen to be making a difference. For classroom teachers, who have spent the day in close confinement with their pupils, this is the last thing they'd think of doing.

Pupils' grasp of time and age is erratic to say the least. When I was in my forties, pupils guessing my age offered suggestions in the 30s, 40s, 50s and even 60s. And they are similarly sketchy in relation to big historical events. I once began a unit on World War I (the play *Journey's End* plus some poetry) with a photocopied extract from my grandfather's diary – the two weeks leading up to the signing of the armistice on the 11 November. He simply recorded: *'11 am hostilities ceased.'* Apart from mentioning a change of billet, the only other word he wrote was *'bath'* – twice. One for each week. Why would he bother to record this, I asked the class. So deeply impressed on their collective consciousness was their History teacher's account of the Nazi concentration camps, that the class immediately connected my grandfather's weekly bath in 1918 with the fake showers in the gas chambers of Auschwitz. When someone else mentioned Hitler by way of explanation I realised it was time to abandon historical context and got on with reading the play.

However hot and uncomfortable it might have been for the last few weeks of the Summer Term, the weather can always be relied upon to change for the worse the minute teachers break up for the long summer **holiday**. Along with the *Back To School* signs in the supermarket, autumn sometimes seems to have its hand on your shoulder even as the summer holiday is starting. Not that you can count on any sympathy from friends and family who work in the real world, who are quick to point out that their entire annual holiday amounts to less than a teacher's summer holiday. Privately teachers would rather compare themselves to their colleagues on the continent or in the independent sector, who enjoy more than just six weeks.

If, as I do, a teacher wants to avoid airports, car hire, crowded beaches and hot nights (literally not metaphorically – teachers tend not to have sex anyway), then a French campsite is one solution for teachers who have children. But cracks are starting to appear in this formula, apart from the obvious drawback of getting roughly the same weather as the UK. Last year one of the legs of our little barbecue was rusted through and as soon as I put the first sausage on the grill the whole thing collapsed and started a camp fire in front of our chalet. Once we'd dampened the flames I marched down to the Eurocamp office seeking a replacement, but it had just shut. As a last resort I borrowed a brand new one from an unoccupied chalet of a rival company.

The next morning an angry rep appeared at our door. 'Is there any reason why you've taken a barbecue belonging to Canvas Holidays?'

Still confined to the tiny bedroom after a night of sickness and diarrhoea I couldn't hear my wife's reply but imagine it involved a frosty glare and the man going on his way.

Our arrival the previous afternoon also hadn't gone quite to plan. What I had thought to be a quiet resort was in fact heaving with people. The swimming pools were especially busy but the lifeguards weren't too busy not to notice I wasn't wearing the regulation speedos. The alarm was raised on their walkie-talkies and shortly after I was run to ground in the children's pool. Swimming shorts, they explained, are less hygienic and so forbidden, and I was sent away to change.

Heavy cloud cover on our second day dramatically reduced the population around the resort and ensured that last year's holiday continued a well-established pattern – arrival in reasonably good weather, heavy rain on our first evening, and then cooler and damper thereafter. Consequently we were queuing up for Monkey World by eleven o'clock on our first morning. My children know their way around the carabines and zip wires and would, I hoped, disappear up into the trees for an hour or so whilst my wife and I could drink coffee and stare into space. Not this year, the instructor informed me cheerfully. The legislation had changed. All children now have to be accompanied by an adult and, despite my precarious condition and lingering dizziness, my wife volunteered me to take to the trees.

In the past I have described this sort of holiday to various people as posh camping but I am beginning to wonder. Last year our plastic mobile home seemed particularly small. One morning when I leant forward, minus my glasses, to lift the toilet seat, I head-butted a low shelf. The shower resembled a tiny plastic pod and spat out painfully hot water if you weren't careful.

There isn't the same pressure to organise how you spend a

half-term holiday, or go anywhere, and consequently these tend to be more relaxing. The Christmas holiday feels like stepping out of the frying pan of the busy Autumn Term and into the fire of Christmas shopping and seeing your relatives, but in half-term the rest of the world is generally still safely at work and you get to enjoy a bit of peace. There is, however, a knack to managing your half-term, which needs to be learned and only comes with experience. As a young teacher just starting out, the relief of not having to go into school can be so great, and a week seems such a wonderfully long barrier from the prospect of work, that the temptation is to indulge yourself too much. The problem is that you end up grinding to a complete, and eventually quite melancholy, halt. Watching foreign films and drinking red wine in the day is good at first, but by Thursday I felt totally miserable and only managed to cheer up after I'd done a couple of days back at school.

I

Inset Days

Intervention

IGCSE

Inappropriate

Inset Days began life in the early 1980s as Baker Days – after Kenneth Baker, one of Mrs Thatcher's Education Secretaries – and before that were originally part of a teacher's holiday. Despite their loss, teachers generally seem much more cheerful and relaxed on Inset Days when the pupils aren't there. Whereas one would imagine that most doctors prefer treating patients to doing paper work, I suspect the majority of teachers secretly prefer the calm, orderly atmosphere and quiet passivity of an Inset Day to actual teaching.

They are generally devoted to professional development, which usually means the dreaded *outside speaker*. One of the last Inset Days I attended was entitled *It's Good To Talk – Communication and Coaching*, harking back to an old BT advert. On the screen in the main hall there was a new slogan below the school badge: *Life-long lovers of learning*. The outside speaker, we were told, was doing us a big favour by coming to speak to us, although was presumably also getting paid, and began with a quote from Lao-Tsu (circa 500 BC) on the nature of *effective leadership*. Apparently the very best leaders aren't noticed, which prompted one of the teachers on my table to mutter something sarcastic under their breath about our previous Headmaster.

Other ideas and phrases in the presentation seemed familiar: the reminder that there were only forty-seven school days until the public exams started in the summer; the frequency with which the outside speaker said *powerful tool*; the *iceberg theory*; the reminder to *fight fire with water*; and *marginal gains* cropped up again, or, as he put it, 'it's all right to tweak'.

The advice on *Active Listening* read to us from the power point included 'make eye contact', 'ask a question' and 'be curious'. The statement of the rather obvious then continued with the speaker's *Three Steps to Assertiveness*. Having 'listened to what the other person is saying' *Step 2* is 'now say what you think'.

The school year usually begins in September with one or sometimes two Inset Days, but just when teachers need to sort out basics like timetables, rooms, making sure new teachers have a desk, keys, stationery and something to teach, Head Teachers still insist on inviting in an outside speaker. Staff tend to be lukewarm about visiting academics and experts in education and resent their tendency to wax lyrical about the joys of teaching from the safety of their research post. Some teachers adopt the truculent attitude of the grumbling foot-soldier, along the lines of 'When was the last time they taught a five period day?' The visiting speaker probably knows this but doesn't let it bother them and often talk on through coffee and beyond it, mixing wry personal anecdote with studied profundity (long reflective pauses) as they lay down the challenge in relation to change and innovation. Being a *catalyst for change* means listening to *opinion leaders* (like them) and a determination to see everything as an *opportunity for learning*.

None of which sounds very appealing and I suspect that I and some of my colleagues are among the *16%* – the *laggards* at the bottom of the food chain.

There's more for staff to do on Inset Days devoted to appraisal or *Performance Management*. Last year's targets have to be reviewed and excuses found, and new (easier) targets have to be set. Bizarrely some colleagues' salaries can be adversely affected by the performance of sixteen year olds in their GCSEs. This impacts mainly on younger teachers, who are still climbing up through the pay thresholds, and so who are especially vulnerable to Senior Management's demands for **intervention** – previously known as more teaching / work – but currently the hottest buzz word of them all. *Intervention, Intervention, Intervention.*

It's hard not to think of legal firms and wealthy partners flogging young lawyers and trainees. Saturday mornings have always been a part of some independent schools, but the teachers in independent schools are better paid and enjoy longer holidays, not to mention better working conditions. It's now spreading to some state schools. They're not called extra lessons, obviously, but *intervention sessions.* Usually intervention sessions take place at the end of the school day, when teachers and pupils are least receptive to spending more time with each other. For a significant number of pupils the last lesson of the day – and for some the one before lunch as well – is one too many, and it's hard to get any real work done. And teachers who've had a full teaching day sometimes find it hard to string a simple sentence together after five or six lessons on the trot. I recall struggling to ask for a book of stamps in the post office straight after one particularly taxing day of teaching.

Intervention generally targets those pupils who are performing below their *Target Grades*, for which there are a number of possible explanations: the Target Grade might not be realistic; the pupil may not do any work at home; and / or has resisted the efforts of their teachers to support them in class. Strangely the solution is to arrange extra teaching for them, or rather *intervention*, just at the time that it has the least chance of being effective.

One method of intervening on a large scale to turn Ds and Es into precious C grades (now 4s and 5s) is the **IGCSE**. The 'I' stands for international. This qualification was previously the preserve of the international jet set, too busy skiing or on their yachts to be bothered with long winded GCSE course work or controlled assessments. A few years ago I attended a training session titled 'Guarantee 90%+ A*-C in English'. A female Head of English described how she had put her relationship on the line in order to turn D grades into C grades. Apparently it was all worth it and made possible by doing the IGCSE. When we tried this with our pupils the next year the loophole had been closed and some of our weaker students experienced a wipe out in the reading paper.

At times a teacher can start to sound like a stuck record asking pupils the rather pointless rhetorical question, 'Do you think that is appropriate?' There's something a bit off-puttingly prim about the word *appropriate* or, more relevantly, ***inappropriate***, but it has a way of cropping up rather a lot during the school day. In a Year 9 lesson on *Othello*, 'He's a batty man' was offered in response to my question about one of the characters. One boy, who had arrived very late to the lesson, attempted to fist bump me and then announced he needed to go to the toilet. 'I'm desperate for a piss, Sir!' At the start of the final period of the day a Year 11 boy I had never spoken to before stopped in the doorway of my classroom, held something out to me and said, 'Smell that'.

Sometimes it is the random act of casual rudeness that hits the teacher hardest. In a lesson with a Year 11 class, just before their mock exams, I interrupted what I was saying about summary technique to remonstrate with two boys on the back row who were stuffing their faces with sweets. I thought I had driven the point home with some force, only to see a boy on the other side of the room nonchalantly eating an orange. He'd dropped all of the peel on the floor and was enjoying his orange seemingly quite oblivious to what I'd just said about eating during lessons.

Even the nicest and brightest pupils can sometimes let you down. One short-lived initiative involved Heads of Department being shadowed by a member of the governing body. My governor was a distinguished ex-local businessman, turned pillar of the community. The lessons he'd attended had gone reasonably well and without incident when, just before the lunch break, in the middle of a discussion about a Jane Austen novel, a sixth former shifted in his seat and let out a resounding fart. My governor smiled indulgently and the lesson continued, just about. Bizarrely the boy betrayed absolutely no embarrassment.

J

Jargon

Jonners

Journey's End

Senior Management have started to use their own language or jargon at staff meetings and it can be hard to keep up. PP, the Pupil Premium grant, is one of Ofsted's, and so also Senior Leadership's, current preoccupations. For this each department will need another Departmental Champion or Ambassador, who will lead on the *top 10 to do action plan* and work to ensure *100% buy-in*. Really important messages like WE ARE THE GATEKEEPERS are delivered in capital letters – it's not only *best practice* – it is *good practice*. Surprisingly, there was still one member of staff sufficiently attentive to query the use of the phrase *open buckets* – apparently the latest jargon to describe subjects other than English and Maths.

There is lots of talk of driving the school forwards – it's all about *going forward*, also *working forward* and *moving forward*. On the big screen are the words *Striving for Excellence*, which are followed by four gold stars. The outside speaker, who has been invited to talk to staff about exciting and dynamic teaching, says that we should be able to just 'watch the plates spin'. Good lessons, apparently 'just go', although there's nothing in their presentation that I could actually imagine using with a class – not clining, nor the register continuum and certainly not nominalisation.

I find myself thinking of **Jonners** on these occasions – a colleague from my first teaching post who scoffed loudly throughout a staff training session on how to send an email. He had read History at Cambridge, always used a fountain pen, often read *The Daily Telegraph* during lessons, and infuriated our Head of Department by playing solitaire on the one PC in the English Office.

Whenever staff meetings got really bad another old colleague would lean towards you conspiratorially and whisper, 'It's all a load of bollocks.'

Having retired, the Art teacher responsible for the Fantasy Absence League, admitted to me that he'd only go back into a classroom if it was at gunpoint, which brought to mind Hibbert, the flaky officer in the play *Journey's End*: *I swear I'll never go into those trenches again. Shoot! – and thank God.* During his teaching career, however, he'd been more like Osborne, the stoical 'uncle' figure. When informed that he will be leading a suicidal raid across No Man's Land, Osborne simply responds with *'Oh. I see.'* He then reassures his superior officer that there's no hard feelings with, *'That's all right, old chap.'* The teacher's life would be so much easier if some of the pupils could acquire a measure of Osborne's self-control, rather than complaining that everything is *long* or *moist*.

Key Stages

Kes

Key Stages now seem rather old hat alongside the current buzz words. They arrived with the National Curriculum, which is rarely mentioned these days, and belong to a time when secondary schools still did SATs and Levels. Both were absolutely fundamental, we were told, to the education of pupils at Key Stage 3 (Years 7-9), but both were scrapped, almost overnight – probably the victims of political tit-for-tat. (The SATs, originally brought in by the Conservatives, were killed off by New Labour, who instead championed Teacher Assessment with Levels, later removed by Gove.) The disappearance of Levels gave rise to a certain amount of soul searching – *Life After Levels* – and the situation which currently exists in secondary schools where each school does its own thing. The only certainty is that pupils will eventually achieve one of the new 1-9 GCSE grades at the end of Year 11, so most schools have hitched their Key Stage 3 waggon to this. They are reluctant to admit that pupils in the lower years might achieve the equivalent of GCSE grades, so often artificially stagger grades (the *journey*) across the years. A grade 2 or 3 at GCSE would be a bit of a disaster for most pupils but in some schools is confusingly awarded to high achieving pupils when they are in Years 7 and 8.

The Year 9 SATs (in English, Maths and Science) were

unceremoniously dumped by New Labour in 2008. One of the problems with public exams is that someone has to mark them and SATs came a poor third after A Levels and GCSEs. Schools were routinely up in arms about the accuracy of the marking. One local school appealed against the marking because it was too generous, with nearly 100% of pupils achieving a Level 5 or better, creating terrifying expectations for their GCSE results further down the line.

Ken Loach's classic film **Kes** still goes down very well with pupils in Key Stage 3. Students empathise with the underdog Billy Casper, are sensitive in relation to his attachment to the kestrel, and genuinely upset at the end when Billy's half-brother Jud kills it and dumps it in a dustbin. However, a number of elements of school life depicted in the film strike pupils as completely alien. Showers after PE or games are especially troubling for some of them. Their attitude to nudity – the prospect of their own and that shown in the film – has them recoiling in horror. Likewise, singing hymns in assembly. They are also shocked by the school's relaxed attitude to school uniform, playing football in goals without nets, the popularity of smoking, and corporal punishment.

L

Learning Walks

Literacy

Learning

Lock Down

As Ofsted inspections have got smaller and smaller, schools have begun inspecting themselves. An alternative to full lesson observations is a **Learning Walk**, which allows members of Senior Management or Heads of Department to see a number of classes in the course of one period.

The problem for the teacher being observed is that this snap shot might well not be the bit of the lesson they'd like the visitor to see. The timing of unannounced visits involves a huge amount of luck and can be cruel. There is the temptation, if they come after the interesting bit of the lesson, simply to rewind and do it again. I once managed to do this for Ofsted with a very obliging A Level group, but further down the school someone is bound to blurt out, 'Haven't we just done this, sir' and give the game away.

Whereas in a lesson observation the observer will probably talk to a number of pupils and look at a sample of their work, my last _Learning Walk_ visitor sat down on the back row next to the least reliable boy in the class, who, of course, had the wrong book and had failed to complete a single piece of work

I had set him that year. The rest of the class played along with the situation, eagerly answering questions, but as soon as the distinguished visitor left, sat back and downed tools and had to be cajoled back to work. Older pupils know what's happening on these occasions and look for signs of stress or meltdown in their teachers. They sometimes burst into ironic applause when the visitor leaves the room, which you hope isn't audible to them as they disappear down the corridor.

When a member of Senior Management wanders into your lesson unannounced you just hope that something reasonably purposeful is going on. Exam preparation can become so tedious that it is sometimes tempting to take a breather and put a film on. A few years ago I succumbed to this temptation and put on *Lock Stock and Two Smoking Barrels* for no obvious educational reason, and incurred the wrath of the KS4 Manager (a PE Teacher), who happened to look in on my class with a message for members of the rugby team.

On another occasion I completely forgot when it was our turn for Departmental Evaluation Week, and was horrified to see the lady in charge of *Teaching and Learning* walk into the room at the start of the lesson. I had banked on spending the lesson reading *Of Mice and Men*, with possibly a bit of the film thrown in at the end. This time I was happy for her to think that she would miss the interesting bit of the lesson where the students actually learnt something – which I wanted to give the impression I was building up to. This was a *Learning Walk*, so she couldn't stay forever, I reasoned, and carried on reading. But rather than move on to another lesson she stayed, and remained for so long that she eventually forced me to show my hand and admit it was going to be one of those reading the book / watching the film lessons.

One *whole school / cross-curricular* initiative involved

walking into lessons in different departments. The timetable for these visits was announced in advance and so I was somewhat surprised at my first stop – a Science lesson – when the teacher showed a video for the duration of my visit. Even more bizarrely, she later sought me out and requested feedback.

The National **Literacy** Strategy, with its reliance on overhead projectors, now seems like ancient history, but was once the newest and shiniest educational initiative in schools – a kind of rebranding exercise for what had been the musty mysteries of English grammar. Not prepared to leave pupils' grasp of the English language to the vagaries of what rubs off from conversation and reading, the literacy strategy took a more proactive approach, demystifying the writing process by means of *scaffolding*, *modelling*, and the reduction of language to *word level*, *sentence level* and *text level*. My Head of Department at the time – probably like most Heads of English – felt we should respond to this by re-writing our schemes of work to accommodate the new terminology. This was before work laptops and as there was no PC in my flat, I spent half of that summer holiday in my friend's bedroom at his computer, devising opportunities to talk about *word level*, *sentence level* and *text level*. I know for a fact that none of my colleagues ever read any of what I produced, let alone used it with a class.

Like most new-fangled subjects – Media Studies, Citizenship, GCSE PE, Business Studies – literacy has a complicated vocabulary for sometimes quite simple concepts. Why are pupils in Year 6, currently being prepared for their KS2 SATs, required to know obscure and pointlessly complicated sounding words like *antonym*? Why can't you just say it's the opposite of something else? And what are *determiners* and where did they come from? Another term Literacy Coordinators are keen on is *nominalisation*. Actually the Wikipedia explanation suggests it's anything but simple – *a part of word formation using a verb / adjective / adverb as a noun, at the head of a noun phrase, with or without morphological transformation, and sometimes requiring the addition of a derivational suffix* – but adds, that it is a *natural part of language*. In other words, like much of English grammar, it's only tricky when you stop and think about it, and more especially when you try and explain it to school children.

Whilst the theory and terminology behind the literacy strategy sounded impressive, the reality of provision in the classroom didn't always match up. In my first school literacy began as a reading period for Year 7. The school had been given a number of book boxes and a hole in the timetable was filled by the introduction of the Reading Period, usually staffed by bored Maths or Design Technology teachers, who were hoping to get some marking done whilst the class read in silence. Whether this fostered a life-long love of reading it's hard to say.

What began as *Teaching and **Learning*** is now starting to be replaced by *Learning and Teaching*, underlining the point that, currently, it's all about *learning*. Either way round it seems an unnecessary slogan to bandy around schools – rather a statement of the obvious for a place of education, like a hospital talking about *healing and curing*. Everything is an *opportunity for learning* and there isn't a minute to lose. So as pupils straggle in to the lesson in dribs and drabs, learning needs to begin immediately. This can be achieved by having a *starter* activity – very often in the form of pictures projected on the whiteboard, accompanied by the hopeful instruction to discuss it with your neighbour. Because learning needs to *begin immediately* it's easy to forget to do the electronic register, which is fast becoming a capital offence. According to Ofsted this is a *safeguarding* issue, and schools have been downgraded from *Good Schools* just because teachers have forgotten to do the register at the start of the lesson, a register, which a few years ago, we weren't required to do anyway.

Another new arrival on the school scene is the **Lock Down Policy**. When we hear five peels of the bell it means we're in *Lock Down* mode. Staff might also be sent a secret code by email to inform them of this, and should then remain where they are. Classrooms are generally designated as the *safe areas*. No one should leave the classroom but teachers should offer sanctuary to any stray pupils wandering the corridors. The government advice for PE teachers doing games out on the school fields is to *'run away'*.

M

(Your) Mum

Of Mice and Men

Music Teachers

For a few years in the late 1990s and early 2000s, *'your mum'* was the standard riposte in any argument, between boys especially. There wasn't usually anything else added to this to explain what 'your mum' may or may not have done or been, but just the implied disrespect of that phrase had pupils running to the teacher in uproar. 'He cussed my mum, sir,' was a constant presence in the classroom and required delicate diplomacy. That was at first, but after a while mums had been mentioned so often that teachers became desensitised, and were liable to respond with, 'I don't care about your mum. Get on with your work.'

Mums continue to be an essential component of the accomplished cusser's tool kit. Two examples in common usage are 'Your mum's a cleaner' and 'Your mum earns £4 an hour'. More cutting still was 'Your mum sold her washing machine to buy your PS3'. All of this despite compulsory Citizenship lessons and assembly topics like Anti-Bullying Week and quotes from Gandhi and the Dalai Lama.

Their creativity in relation to cussing probably stems, in large part, from boredom, and when it comes to situations requiring real sensitivity pupils tend to pass with flying colours. *Mums* were unfortunately mentioned in a class of low ability Year 9 boys I was teaching at the end of the morning about twenty years ago. The class had forgotten that one of the boys had recently lost his mother. The boy said nothing but put his head down on the table. The class immediately understood. One of them went over to him and patted him on the shoulder and asked if he was ok. They then worked in respectful silence for the remainder of the lesson.

And as much as pupils enjoy taking the mickey out of each other, they tend to be much more sensitive and generous to those they regard as hard done by or underdogs. In fiction this includes Billy Casper (*Kes*), Tom Robinson (*To Kill A Mockingbird*), Piggy (*Lord of the Flies*), Joe Gargery and Magwitch (*Great Expectations*), Boxer (*Animal Farm*), and Lennie in **Of Mice and Men**.

Of Mice and Men remains an essential rite of passage for any secondary school pupil, although, as it's no longer a GCSE exam text, students are more likely to encounter it in Year 9. Presumably this makes it more likely that other pupils will innocently repeat my own schoolboy error, reading 'whorehouse' as war house, much to the delight, as I recall, of everyone else in the class. It remains the one novel that always manages to engage and / or pacify even the most difficult classes and English teachers have always resisted any change to the syllabus which doesn't include it as one of the set texts. Its advantages, briefly, are: it consists mainly of dialogue (pupils become restless during long passages of description) and there's the chance to do American accents and a funny voice for Lennie; there's a memorable fight scene in which the obnoxious son of the boss (Curley) has his hand crushed by lovable Lennie; the plight of the weak characters – Lennie, old Candy, Candy's dog, Crooks and eventually Curley's wife – touches pupils emotionally; there's a frank analysis of the respective merits of the local brothels; and it's mercifully short. It was a dark day when the exam board replaced it for a period with Hemingway's *The Old Man and the Sea*, which has no advantages for the teacher, and virtually none for the reader. Not surprisingly for a novel which largely depicts a man fishing, there also isn't a good film version available. The one I did find was so bad that students opted to read the book instead.

If children are growing up too quickly these days, studying *Of Mice and Men* in Key Stage 3 rather than for GCSE, isn't going to help, what with Curley's *'Glove fulla vaseline'*, George's assessment of a man's needs (*'give me a good whore house every time…a guy can go in an' get drunk and get ever'thing outta his system all at once'*), the terrible treatment of the black stable buck Crooks, and the bleak pessimism of the ending. But pupils genuinely love the book.

Michael Gove, however, apparently doesn't. *The Independent* reported in 2014 that he *'really dislikes'* it, before adding that it had been *'studied by 90% of the teenagers taking English Literature in the past'*. According to *The Sunday Times* Gove thinks that *'students ought to focus on works by British writers such as Jane Austen and Shakespeare'*. It also quoted a Senior Lecturer at King's College, London, who described the new specification as *'a syllabus out of the 1940s…rumour has it Mr Gove, who read Literature, designed it himself…This will just grind children down'*.

There's always been an element of grind about the push in Year 11 towards GCSEs – lots of different subjects making demands on pupils and ratchetting up the pressure – but the addition of Govian favourites like Romantic Poetry and the compulsory pre-20th century novel has made it worse in

English Literature. The inclusion of the confusing *structure* question in the GCSE English Language exam also makes life much more difficult for everybody – the equivalent, with most pupils, of teaching tricks like the rabona to non-footballers, or what some PE teachers used to refer to, unofficially, as 'the flower arrangers'. It is a specialist question which would flummox most members of staff, and has become another source of discouragement to pupils thinking of continuing with English at A Level and beyond.

Music teachers generally fall into two categories. There are the affable musicians, who would really prefer the precarious life of the musician, if it wasn't for the fact that they have to pay the mortgage. They tend not to seek high office, or become *Directors of Music*, but preserve a fairly low profile and go under the radar of Senior Management. It is another sort of Music teacher who becomes the Director of Music, and promises to have every pupil learning an instrument or singing in a choir. These are the prickly showmen, often in the mould of TV choirmaster Gareth Malone, who are good at getting their own way, and sometimes even aspire to become members of the Senior Management, although this doesn't happen very often.

The two Music teachers at my school definitely fell into these contrasting camps – kindly old Mr Birkenshaw, who played us selected pieces of classical music from his collection of *Deutsche Grammophon* records, and occasionally let us make some noise with an assortment of hand held percussion instruments, and his more extrovert colleague and Head of Department, Mr Wedgewood. He also encouraged the use of his Christian name and was universally addressed as Cyril. Cyril's job, as far as he was concerned and as he explained frequently to his pupils, was putting on concerts and shows, and they could hardly expect him to do the teaching as well. When a parent complained that his Year 8 class had spent the Autumn Term moving chairs or waiting for Cyril to show up for their lesson, he retaliated in the next lesson, very pointedly dictating several sides on the life of Mozart.

On one occasion Cyril whispered a lecherous and totally inappropriate breast-related comment about a young female teacher doing the Lower School assembly, much to the delight of the Year 8 boys at the back of the hall, who, as one, burst out laughing. After the assembly the understandably angry female teacher asked a boy in my class called Headley-Smith why they had been laughing. In a panic he shared the precise wording of Cyril's comment and Cyril was hauled in to explain himself to the Head. In our next music lesson Cyril was late showing up as he usually was, but when he did arrive something about his manner prompted our class to fall silent. He strode menacingly over to the bookshelf, took down *The Oxford Companion to Music*, and hurled it across the room towards Headley-Smith, who was leaning back on his chair. It struck Headley-Smith full on the side of his head and knocked him off his chair. Cyril then delivered a furious tirade, to the effect of what goes on tour, stays on tour.

In my first teaching post the two male Music teachers were divided by geography as well as temperament. They disliked each other so much that they had to be housed on different sites – one had his classroom at the upper school and one at the lower. Rather like Cyril, the Head of Department wasn't very interested in teaching, and had lots of freelance engagements in London to juggle his teaching around. His estranged colleague – the 'affable musician' – was a fantastic musician but wasn't at all affable, and couldn't stand the sight of children. Unsurprisingly music wasn't exactly flourishing. This was all to change with the arrival of a young, thrusting Director of Music and committed colleagues. Also the affordability of electronic keyboards and, importantly, headphones, meant that pupils could actually make some music that wasn't on a triangle or tambourine.

N

Newly Qualified Teachers (NQTs)

Nicknames

My first year as a teacher fortunately coincided with the gap between what was called the *probation year*, with its unfortunate undertones of custodial sentences and judicial procedure, and what has become the year of being an **NQT** – a Newly Qualified Teacher. As a result there were far fewer hoops to jump through, and there wasn't the threat of not passing. I was, however, required to attend the borough meetings for new teachers. The borough advisers provided courgette quiche and a confessional atmosphere in which we could share our various mishaps in the classroom. (Mine included locking myself and the class out of the room when my HOD came to observe me teach for the first time. Nobody could find the caretaker and much of the lesson was spent in the corridor.) On arrival we were given a sheet depicting monkeys in various stages of climbing a tree and asked to colour in the monkey we most related to after half a term of teaching – the one hanging on by their finger tips from the lowest branches or the smug ape at the top of the tree.

This was my first exposure to the rather nebulous role and contribution of borough advisers. Later, as an experienced teacher, I attended the borough's 'training' for a new GCSE specification. There were only four of us but the 'trainer' asked us to get into two groups and discuss something they'd written on the flipchart. They then strung out the process of feeding back for forty five minutes and that was it, our training. And when a school experiences an unsuccessful Ofsted it is an opportunity for the borough advisers to descend on that school like a colony of vultures – to support the process of recovery, justify their existence, and later claim credit for helping to turn the school round and upwards to a better Ofsted inspection.

Although there is the possibility that an NQT has no idea what they are doing, they possess a number of advantages and are therefore popular with Head Teachers. They are obviously cheaper than more experienced teachers. They tend to be more up on and more enthusiastic about the latest educational initiatives. And they usually work their socks off and are unlikely to rock the boat by questioning the school's management.

When I started as a new teacher in my first school, as well as learning the names of my pupils and colleagues, I also had to put a name to Tuck-box, Spud, The Mole, Bomber, Sir Les, Whispering Pat, Mad Jack, Smurf, The Nook, Meekon, Boom Boom and The Moose. Some of these **nicknames** were known only to members of staff, but others, like The Moose, or my own (Egon, from the film *Ghostbusters*), were common currency between the pupils and often heard shouted down corridors behind the teacher's back.

But in recent years nicknames seem to have rather died out. Along with the lanyards most of the staff wear around their neck, the teaching version of corporate professionalism dictates that we refer to each other as *Sir* or *Miss*. The use of Christian names in front of the pupils has always been a bit of a grey area, but now the use of Sir and Miss has spread to the staff room and private conversations with other members of staff. Perhaps it's another example of professional wishful thinking,

like addressing a difficult group of boys as *gentlemen,* in the
hope that they might take this to heart and behave a bit better.

O

Ofsted

Outstanding

Open Evenings

Teachers used to really know when an **Ofsted** Inspection was taking place. The inspectors arrived in large numbers and took over a designated room or wing of the school, as well as most of the parking spaces. The fact that most of their cars were superior models to those of the staff, added to the teachers' sense of injustice. Schools were also given about three months advanced warning in which to prepare / stage manage / second guess every facet of the week long inspection. My third Ofsted Inspection was scheduled for the week after the October half-term, which encouraged teachers to attempt a completely unsustainable amount of preparation. The inspectors were obviously aware of this, were extra conservative in their judgements of lessons, and the overall judgement of the school obstinately remained the same – *Good*.

One Head Teacher, knowing that Ofsted were due at some point in the spring or early summer, insisted on teachers writing formal lesson plans for all of their lessons from the start of January. When the inspector walked in we were to produce our file of detailed and up-to-date lesson plans. Having failed to keep up with this during the first half of the Spring Term I set about writing them retrospectively during the February half-term, only to end up having to scrap the first attempt and write them all again because I had slipped into the past tense, which rather gave the game away. The school's lesson planning sheet required us to state *Aims & Objectives* – in two separate boxes. Separating the two was a thorny issue on the PGCSE course – the course tutor insisted they were different – and remained a point of confusion and a horrible waste of time at the start of each lesson plan. (The dictionary defines an *aim* as the 'the object at which something is aimed' and an *objective* as 'of or relating to a goal or aim'.)

The move to short notice inspections gave rise to stories of staff staying at school long into the night and of Head Teachers sending out for takeaway pizza to keep them going. Now inspections are short notice (twenty-four hours) and of short and fairly painless duration, from the classroom teacher's point of view at least. This presumably saves lots of money but requires Senior Managers to do the inspecting themselves. Central to this is the *SEF* – the school's Self-evaluation Form – which on-the-ball Heads are constantly updating and collecting evidence for.

This fundamental shift – towards telling Ofsted what you want them to hear, rather than them taking the time to find out the facts for themselves – has taken place in the last ten years or so. In the 1990s and early 2000s your subject inspector stuck to the Head of Department like glue, often requesting extra meetings before and after school. By the end of the week you were sick of the sight of them, but you could usually bring yourself to acknowledge that they had earned the right to their opinion on the work your department was doing. These one-to-one meetings were then watered down to a meeting between an inspector and the Heads of English, Maths, and Science, and then, in the following inspection, to a twenty minute meeting between an inspector, who arrived late, and six assorted Heads of Department, who he invited to tell him things which he wrote down, without question or challenge. It didn't take us long to catch on and by the end of the meeting we were outlining a host of outlandish enrichment opportunities, and were, in short, *outstanding*. The judgement, however, remained *Good*.

An **Outstanding** judgement from Ofsted is now the prize, and once achieved will usually be accompanied by a banner proclaiming the fact, positioned somewhere on the outside of the school premises, where motorists and passers-by can see it. These range in price between about £40 up to nearly £300 and there are a growing number of suppliers to choose from. A primary school, which received a *Good* judgement from Ofsted, bucked this trend by displaying a banner which read *Not Outstanding Yet*.

However, like acquiring a Michelin Star, becoming *Outstanding* creates new pressures – specifically how to stay *Outstanding* and retain the weary staff who got the school there. It might be a more realistic policy just to settle for *Good*. In a *Good* school Ofsted say that *'Teachers have high expectations'*, which is fair enough and true for the vast majority of teachers. In an *Outstanding* school *'All teachers have consistently high expectations of all pupils'*. This would have immediately disqualified my first school – a very good school – because quite a few of the older hands, when asked what they taught, liked to answer 'bastards'. A doctor isn't expected to tell 'all' of their patients that they have 'high expectations' of them all pulling through a dangerous illness, if in fact they believe there is very little chance of them surviving. Why should teachers have 'high expectations' for all of their pupils, when the evidence to the contrary might be so depressingly obvious.

Another of Ofsted's seven criteria for outstanding teaching is that *'Teachers systematically and effectively check pupils' understanding throughout lessons, anticipating when they need to intervene and doing so with notable impact on the quality of the learning.'* The relentlessness of the language and tone – *'systematically'*, *'effectively'*, *'notable impact'* – is annoying but there's also something about the rhythm of this sentence which sounds like Michael Gove or the voice over on an exam board assessment and moderation video. Ofsted seem to envisage the teacher in the mould of attentive aide de camp, or butler, a shadow behind their master's chair, ready to step forward and refill a glass or clear their plate. The servile aspect of this is irritating and also the rather fanciful notion that teachers need to silently 'anticipate' where there are problems – as if pupils don't tell the teacher very loudly the instant they are confused ('I don't get this sir / miss. This is moist.') Notwithstanding the pupils' resistance to learning something the first time round, the teacher then swoops (*'intervenes'*) with *'notable impact'* to save the day. If only it was that straightforward.

In the flesh Ofsted inspectors have generally been reasonable in the way they have applied the criteria and have understood that it isn't possible to do everything. But at the margins there is money to be made, and a multitude of websites and technology-based education solutions stoke up Ofsted angst whilst simultaneously promising to solve it. These are usually keen on *Personalised Learning*, and while acknowledging that this may sound arduous, suggest that teachers create a *Learning Log* – and use their technology to create a *Learner Journey e-portfolio* so that pupils can *'document the milestones in their learning'*. The key is to *'show how they're progressing and how close they are to achieving their goals.'* Pupils have all sorts of goals and ambitions, but they don't usually involve keeping a record of their learning at school.

One educational service offers a *'free lesson recording demo'* so that teachers can show the inspector not just their lesson plans, but all of their previous lessons as well. This would have come in handy a few years ago when an Ofsted inspector came to observe me during period one with a small A level group. It's fair to say that this particular Year 13 group weren't quite so bothered about the inspection as their teachers. Five minutes after the bell had sounded for the start of the lesson, only one of them had shown-up. I looked at the inspector as if to say what do you want me to do? Video footage of previous lessons would at least have proved the existence of the other members of the class, who then arrived at five minute intervals for the first twenty-five minutes of the lesson. Not quite the clean start I was looking for or *learning* beginning immediately.

Open Evening, or Prospective Parents' Evening, usually takes place in October, and has become an increasingly important date in the school calendar, both for schools and parents. Traditionally it was for the parents of children in their last year at primary school (Year 6) but is now also attended by parents of pupils in Year 5 and even Year 4. It doesn't do a school's reputation any good to be undersubscribed and this is their chance to put on a show. This used to come in the form of bubbling chemicals and explosions, or dissected rats in the science labs, or beat the goalie in the sports hall. This is still on the menu but is secondary to the Head Teacher's address to parents in the main hall. Key messages to do with student welfare, progress and opportunity will be conveyed in a carefully choreographed presentation, now often accompanied by a short film, student speakers, and / or a choir, all celebrating achievement in the school.

For ordinary teachers, given the afternoon off to freshen up displays in their classrooms, it's a more humdrum experience. Changing the date on the display is the easiest labour saving device.

English teachers have to accept that a room full of books and the pupils' written work isn't one of the hotter attractions on the tour, and we usually have a fairly quiet night. Most of the interest comes from parents in the form of nostalgia for the long lost texts of their school days. '*An Inspector Calls!* I read that.' Rather alarmingly primary school children have started asking questions like 'What challenge will you be able to provide if I come here?'

Last year three members of one family of four managed to irritate me in the space of a couple of minutes. The father asked a succession of particularly redundant questions – 'Is this what the classroom will look like?' – whilst his daughter scribbled on my desk. And then my conversation with the mother was interrupted by her ten year old son barking 'Why have you got a lap top and a PC?' When I didn't immediately respond he said, 'I don't want to come here anyway. It's rubbish.'

P

PIXL Club

Parring

Poetry

Plenaries

Pride and Prejudice

Parents' Evenings

Pushy Parents

PE Teachers

Photographs

Pastries

Despite the obvious determination of the Tories to depress GCSE grades – that is until they introduced their new specifications and number grades in 2017 – schools have continued to fight valiantly to reproduce the sort of grades they'd managed under New Labour. One organisation which offers assistance to this end is **PiXL,** who invite schools to join the *club* as *partners in excellence*, committed to achieving the *highest outcomes*. PiXL describes itself as a *not-for-profit partnership*, but it still costs schools over £3000 to join the *PiXL Club* or *family*.

Something about the silly name put me off PiXL from the start but in the end I buckled to pressure from my Head Teacher and Line Manager and attended a PiXL Club meeting. The atmosphere in the conference hall resembled an evangelical church or a meeting of the Moonies – which I should have anticipated from an organisation which claims to be *driven by a deep moral purpose*. Ranks of teachers (converts) sat grinning imbecilically, whilst the grandee, who was the founder of PiXL, gave his welcome. At one point two members of the audience stood up and role played a scripted conversation – to model the sort of conversation I should be having with my opposite number, the Head of Maths, when I got to school the following day. There was also mention of the PiXL Choir, which had just been created to help *celebrate achievement*.

PiXL claims not to be *driven by soundbites* but isn't averse to the odd slogan. Its latest initiative is a *character development programme* called *The Edge*, and everything seems to revolve around what it calls *The 3Cs: Culture, Character and* (hard?) *Currency*.

The real currency amongst some of my pupils, the thing which gives them the 'edge' over their classmates, is what they've taken to referring to as **parring** – otherwise known as the exchange of verbal insults. Whilst some pupils may show no capacity for creative reading – for making links and seeing connections – in matters of parring or cussing they can be exceptionally associative in their thinking. It's hard not to admire their creativity and quickness of thinking, even if it's only used to take the mick. At one point during a lesson on pathetic fallacy with a difficult Year 10 class studying *Great Expectations* – in which the concept had been reduced to something like 'light is good' and 'dark is bad' – a pupil asked me to repeat what I'd just said. Something in his expression made me smell a rat, and sure enough, something in the words I'd used had inadvertently parred a boy in the row in front of him.

With this particular class it was necessary to avoid a whole catalogue of potentially incendiary words and phrases, all of which the class would have pounced on and directed to the relevant member of the class. It was even necessary to side-step the word 'head' and related matters. 'Brain' was also a no go area, and greeted with an outbreak of parring aimed at the head shape of one of the boys in the class. Foolishly I tried introducing this class to a **poem** by Simon Armitage called *About His Person*, which consists of a succession of clues and metaphors which reveal the fate of the 'person' (presumably corpse) to whom the various objects mentioned belong. They were then required to write their re-creation – a sequence of rhyming couplets detailing what would be 'about the person' of their choice. I suggested a famous person or figure from history as their subject, but unwisely gave in to their requests to base it on other members of the class – and so, unwittingly, gave my blessing to an exercise in parring their neighbour. The five minutes at the end of the lesson (my **plenary**) were devoted to sharing aloud a collection of provocative personal insults, mainly revolving, it seemed, around head shape.

The other big preoccupation and source of ammunition is weight. One boy interrupted the BBC version of ***Pride and Prejudice*** to denounce a boy on the back row as an 'obese panda'. I stopped the film and asked him to go to the Duty Manager, which he did very slowly and via an altercation with a boy in the front row, which required him to be physically restrained and escorted the rest of the way. When I explained to the Duty Manager, after the lesson, that he'd called another boy 'obese' he flatly denied it.

'No I didn't, I swear!'

This went back and forth for a bit until I repeated the charge a fifth time ('I distinctly heard you call him obese') – and the boy shouted back in exasperation, 'I did not call him a beast.'

The Duty Manager looked at me pityingly from beneath raised eyebrows, awaiting my next move, which was to spell out o-b-e-s-e. 'Did you call him an obese panda?'

'Yes sir.'

But the storm had passed – our combined indignation disarmed by farce and confusion.

Unwisely I took this boy's class out in to the playground in the Summer Term to play a game of cricket. Unfortunately, members of the public walking past the school kept stopping to watch the game from the other side of the playground fence, from where they could also hear the constant stream of abuse being exchanged on the field of play. This was hardly a great advert for the school so I did my best to contain it by moving antagonistic members of the fielding team as far away from each other as possible. But when the non-striking batsmen berated the bowler for being too fat at the top of his voice, I thought I had no choice but to make an example of him in front of the watching public and so terminated his innings and sent him back to his team mates sitting by the fence, from where, unfortunately, his subsequent outbursts and bad language were even more audible to the spectators.

The parring isn't always necessarily verbal. One Year 9 class ended with a bang and me wrestling a furious boy from the room in order to prevent him from murdering one of his classmates. The provocation – someone sticking a post-it note on his back containing an unflattering text – caused a violent transformation in a usually polite pupil. Having hurled two desks out of his way, he sprinted towards the front of the room in pursuit of his tormentor. *Intervention* comes in many forms and this resembled a desperate struggle with an enormous fish. With some difficulty I managed to bundle him out into the corridor and on to the Duty Manager's room, where upon he sat down and burst into tears.

When I returned to the classroom I found one of the nicest pupils in the class picking up shards of plastic from the floor – the shattered remains of a ceiling tile destroyed by a high flying basketball in the two minutes I had been out of the room. Feeling the need to share this extra indignity with someone else, I went and got the Duty Manager. We stood shaking our heads at the damage, whilst the look on his face seemed to say – not for the first time that year – thanks for giving me more work to do.

Parents evenings should, in theory, be a chance for the teacher to get their own back on unruly and uncooperative pupils. Occasionally it's nice to make a difficult pupil squirm in front of their parents, but the worst offenders aren't usually the squirming sort. If you paint too black a picture of the child's behaviour (i.e. tell the truth) it begs the questions why you haven't taken steps to sort it out earlier in the year – or, in current jargon, why you haven't *put strategies in place to support the pupil's learning.* Or you can simply look weak in front of their parents, and the pupils, who now routinely attend parents' evening.

The early phone call home can also hit snags. On one occasion the phrase 'I am very unhappy with her behaviour' was received as me being 'very happy with her behaviour' because the mum's English wasn't very good. I had to cut short her expressions of thanks with the bad news, and came off the phone regretting having made the call. Sometimes parents'

English is so poor that they can't really understand anything the teacher is telling them at parents' evening. Once this becomes apparent, and if their child isn't there to translate, it's time for 'They're doing very well' and the parting handshake.

Native speaker tradesmen offer a different sort of challenge. In my second year of teaching I went on for ages about a Year 9 boy's erratic responses to the Shakespeare play he was studying for his SATs exam, only for his dad – shortly to become my plumber – to lean back in his plastic chair, fold his arms, and declare, 'Yeah well, Ashley likes a laugh.'

Parents aren't always prepared to face up to the reality of their child's performance at school. After sitting her AS exam at the start of June, one girl vanished. She didn't attend a single lesson, was introduced to none of the reading for the summer holiday, and I assumed and had rather hoped that was the last we'd see of her. When I pointed some of this out to her mum at Parents' Evening the following September, she took me to task. 'We're not going to start the year with negatives Mr…erm? We are going to be positive, aren't we Maddie.'

There's usually one parent who you dread seeing and being grilled by. One such, who was referred to amongst my colleagues as Mr Angry, carried an air of menace and a long list of grievances against his son's teachers, who had let him down (again). Even his wife seemed to dislike him and I used to find myself talking more to her to avoid his intense stare.

'How do we know that the guidance you're giving our son is giving him the best chance to achieve an A grade? Clearly something has gone wrong.'

His son had achieved a C grade. I was conscious of my colleague at the next desk following the drama with a keen ear and enjoying my discomfort, and was keen to end the conversation. I promised to make the boy work even harder and predicted greater success in the summer. After some head shaking Mr Angry departed with a look that said, 'I'll be holding you to that.'

A measure of the entitlement presumably felt by parents whose children attend fee paying schools is starting to rub off on some of the parents of children in state schools. This isn't surprising given that the Conservative Government is doing its best to make state schools look like independent schools. And once some parents see an inflated aspirational *Target Grade* they sniff accountability and want an explanation if it isn't achieved.

Most parents patiently submit to the organised chaos of Parents' Evenings, and accept the long waits with the same quiet stoicism of patients in a doctor's waiting room. Occasionally **pushy parents** will try to jump in before it's their turn, leaving the teacher to sort out who is the rightful next customer. Teachers are often also anxious to get through their appointments quickly and tend to discourage pupils from booking the later slots. Sometimes it's possible for teachers to intercept parents unsure of which teacher to see next, a sort of gazumping manoeuvre achieved by establishing eye contact, standing up and waving, and on occasions by physically approaching parents before they head off to see the Maths teacher.

Last year when I moved on from ***Pride and Prejudice*** to the obligatory exam board **poetry** anthology, one of the class responded with 'What's this shit?' as soon as he realised that the book on his desk contained poetry. This is a variation on groaning or the 'Poetry is gay' attitude engraved on the desk in the sports hall, but conveys the immediate response of most pupils towards poetry. The wonder is that they buckle down and apply themselves to what is hardly the most vital part of their education. RE (which is also widely dismissed as being 'gay') fares even worse than poetry, which has always struck me as very unfair – the big world religions and belief systems that impact on the world we live in, versus the poetic expression of one individual.

In a Year 10 poetry lesson a pupil, who had asked for help, dissolved into laughter as soon as I began my explanation. A few minutes later another student asked for help – I suspect prompted by the first pupil – and I noticed I was being watched by him and his neighbour from across the other side of the room. Both seemed to find something very amusing. Pupils find all sorts of ways to avoid the tedium of studying poetry and I imagine this was just another way to get through a lesson on Larkin's *The Whitsun Weddings*.

An alternative to explaining the poem yourself is the *GCSEPod* – a library of online talking tutorials, which have a strangely calming effect on pupils, I suspect because they are, in parts, extremely boring. But they can come to your aid with poems you might otherwise avoid. Robert Browning's poem *My Last Duchess* was one from the anthology that I and the class had taken an instant dislike to. They had declared it to be *'long'* – which it is – but it was also one of their favourite expressions for everything. I just didn't understand it but the *GCSEPod*, fortunately, explained what it was all about and it was negotiated without too much difficulty.

No one needs a *GCSEPod* to help them play or teach ping pong, and every time I walk past the school hall, where pupils are playing table tennis in their **PE** lesson, under the supervision of a teacher who is engrossed in their lap top (it used to be a tabloid newspaper or a copy of *Racing Post*), I experience dark thoughts about the unfairness of life. All of the students are happily on task and what's more there will be nothing for the teacher to mark at the end of the lesson. Put the tables away and that's that.

I doubt I am the only teacher of an academic subject having these resentful thoughts. Without marking or much in the way of lesson planning to hinder their progress, PE teachers tend to climb through the ranks quicker than their colleagues in other departments, and are usually very well represented at Senior Management level. At one point at my last school over half of the senior leadership team had originated as PE teachers. Crowd control, a booming voice which will carry across the sports' field, and the ability to be nasty / scary when required, also tends to be in the PE teachers armoury, and gives them an advantage when it comes to getting jobs as a Year Manager – an essential staging post on the career path to Senior Leadership.

PE teachers are often also required to teach an academic subject to the lower years. This isn't always Geography but generally involves a text book. My own love affair with mathematics began in my first year (Year 7) at secondary school under the fearsome Mr Hooker, a PE teacher who took us for Maths and played scrum half for London Scottish at the weekend. Instead of a dunce hat, Mr Hooker awarded his weaker students (like me) a scrum cap to wear as a dubious badge of honour – a very public mark of their lack of distinction. The following year, when we had the quietly spoken Mr Nolan, whom we nicknamed *the Lurcher*, we could hear Mr Hooker in the next classroom berating his unfortunate Year 8 class, bellowing unflattering comparisons with some of the boys in our class. 'God boy, you're even thicker than Thompson!'

Mr Hooker did have a more caring side but was careful not to let it show. He arrived at one of our Maths lessons carrying an iron bar, which he brought crashing down on the desks of the front row, inches from the boys' fingers. An alternative to the scrum cap treatment was the *no-thought bubble* – which he drew on the board and stood boys up against whenever they got anything badly wrong. Next to the bubble was an arrow and the label *Idiot*.

Putting the fear of God into the new arrivals is part of the PE teachers' traditional methodology. At my first school the Year 7's first PE lesson consisted of a 'getting a few things straight' talk from the members of the PE Department. Whilst the boys sat nervously in rows, the PE teachers stood at the front of the gymnasium in their tight shorts, with their arms folded staring at the boys with apparent hostility. Eventually one of them would step forward and introduce his scary colleagues, along the lines of, 'This is Mr Moxon. This is him in a good mood. I won't tell you what he's like when he's in a bad mood. Some of you will find out soon enough. My name's Mr Back. I am not your friend. I don't want you to send me a Christmas card or remember my birthday. I don't even want you to say good morning to me. I don't want you to say anything to me. Got it?'

This had the desired effect of silencing the many questions and general neediness of the new Year 7 pupils. In academic lessons, where these sort of strong arm tactics don't tend to be used, the teacher has to provide constant clarification and reassurance – 'How long should it be sir?', 'Can we write on the back of the paper sir?', 'Shall I go on to the next page sir?'

On the down side, the shelf life of a PE teacher is shorter than their academic colleagues and is, perhaps, another reason why more PE teachers end up on Senior Management. They don't look so good in their shorts and track suits once they move into middle age, and so are happy to swap them for a seat on the board. One of my old colleagues – a former Head of PE – who didn't go down the Senior Management route, succumbed instead to boredom and became a gloomy presence in the staff room, often heard complaining about colleagues who hadn't refilled the kettle after they'd made themselves a cup of tea. He left teaching and cheered up almost immediately. After a brief and unsuccessful flirtation with welding he went on to do shift work at a local pharmaceutical manufacturer. It was his job to watch the jars trundling along the conveyor belt to see if any of the lids were not on properly, and he was reportedly much happier doing this than teaching.

School **photographs** are now taken at the start of the year so that *SIMS* (School Information Management System) can be updated. This means that teachers often have photographs of the pupils in their classes before they meet them – a definite advantage in the sense of knowing your enemy and their names before you meet them – and can have a seating plan in place for their first lesson.

Before *SIMS* it was possible to get caught out at Parents' Evening if you hadn't managed to put a name to all of the faces in your class, but now there's no excuse for teachers not knowing who they're talking about.

Later in the year there are photos of the different year groups. Pupils are arranged in size order on steep metal steps. Amassed in one body students enjoy a powerful combination of unity and anonymity, and tend to play up accordingly. Even though the photographer may be miked up they can struggle to make themselves heard above the din. 'Hands down' is usually the main issue for the photographer and teachers in attendance are required to point out any rude gestures. Each time a culprit is taken to task there are loud boos and jeers. Sat in the front row with their entire year group behind them, there's not much the Year Head can do about behaviour. In my second year of teaching a whole school photograph was taken in the school field. Something was thrown and landed down the opening of a female Geography teacher's blouse. She stood up and faced the massed ranks and unwisely demanded, *'Who threw that?'* More boos and jeers and not surprisingly no one came forward and confessed.

One way of galvanising staff and fortifying them against the rigours of the school day is to provide **pastries** in the staff room. Last year an email came round announcing, *'Get that Friday feeling with a pastry!!!'* Later in the year it was announced, in an email titled *Sugar rush*, that the Friday treat would be extended to the whole of the last week before half-term because everyone was knackered. Members of Senior Management and even some teachers seem to embrace this breathless, 'let's all work flat out until we're on our knees' culture, and sometimes compare their levels of tiredness, like soldiers comparing war wounds, as if it's a badge of honour.

A young teacher, who joined the school last year, told me that the Head of Department at her previous school had advised her to buy or rent a flat closer to the school so that she could keep on top of the job. The Head of Department had apparently taken her junior colleague to an upstairs window, pointed at a nearby building, and said smugly, 'That's where I live.'

Questions

According to an article in the *TES* (*Times Educational Supplement*) teachers ask two **questions** every minute, as many as four hundred a day, seventy thousand in a year, and between two and three million in the course of their career. With one particularly difficult GCSE group I had to repeat every question two or three times in order to get any response and by the end of the year had lost the fog horn setting in my voice, which the teacher sometimes relies on to clear the room or startle the class to attention. An Ear, Nose and Throat specialist confirmed that I had a slight voice strain. My appointment only lasted a few minutes and there was no mention of rest and relaxation and any time off work. Having put a tiny camera up my nose, the consultant asked me to stick my tongue out, keep it out whilst closing my mouth, puff out my cheeks and say *'eeeh'*. He then modelled the restrained vocal pitch I should have been using in the classroom.

The *TES* article also mentions that *'if you've been teaching for around fourteen and a half years you could be about to ask your one millionth question'*. Some educational websites encourage teachers to keep a record of their questions, which opens up the possibility in the future of ultra-professional teachers knowing when they are honing in on the big milestones – thousandth, ten thousandth, millionth question etc – like a shop welcoming their millionth customer. It could be another opportunity to *celebrate achievement* – yours and theirs – but what if the pupil makes a mess of it and gives a dud answer to your millionth question. There is always that possibility.

Children's main fear, apparently, is not getting the answer wrong but of looking silly, which of course has its own special name – *peer fear*. Perhaps it was this that froze me in the headlights of one of Mr Hooker's questions, and made me blurt out 'Two' as the answer to his question, 'What's 1 x 1?' As I recall this wasn't a question he put to the whole class. He didn't bother with *Pose, Pause & Pounce* (or *Bounce* which is sometimes listed as an extra stage) but went straight for me *(pounce)* and then, to help me with my learning, hit me over the head with a text book whilst repeating the mathematical principle which I had ignored. Perhaps Mr Hooker's approach satisfied this well-known educational slogan – *Good teaching starts with questions not answers* – but even with my low level of attainment in Maths, his question couldn't be described as the kind of high level, open question likely to inspire deeper learning.

At some point during a *Teaching and Learning* meeting or Inset training on *effective questioning*, Bloom's *Taxonomy* will be mentioned. I, and I imagine quite a few of my colleagues, will try to adopt a facial expression which gives off the appearance of recognition and understanding, but somehow I will find myself switching off, and so fail to grasp what it's all about, yet again. From what I have gathered, Bloom's *Taxonomy* seems to be used to make quite a simple thing, like asking questions, feel much more complicated. This is a favourite pastime of educational academics, and there is nothing which can't be formalised. The website Teacher Tools, for example, provides *'types of question'* for *'classroom questioning in English'*. In case the teacher is having a bad day and can't manage to formulate a question on pupils' *knowledge* or *comprehension* they suggest the wording *'Why did'* or *'what happened when?'* And for *evaluation* you could begin with *'What do you think of…?'* As well as helpful wording there are generic definitions for different types of question – *Key, Signal, Fat, Skinny* etc – and a multitude of teaching methods – *Basketball questioning, Conscripts & Volunteers, Phone a Friend, hot seating* and *mantle the expert*, for which presumably you need a cloak. Inevitably there are also question-related acrostic abbreviations – *CLAPS* (context, language, audience, purpose, style), *DEAL* (describe, explain, analyse, link), *IWWM* (in what way might), plus the *5Ws* (who, what, where, when, why). Alternatively you can just ask the questions most pertinent to what you are doing with the class.

R

Reading

Recruitment

Reports

Resilience

Results Day

Whilst teachers are busy encouraging **reading** – this can involve dressing up as a fictional character to celebrate *World Book Day* – the majority of pupils have other commitments which prevent them completing reading at home – their phones, their X-box / PS3, their social life, sleep, etc. Even in class it can run into difficulties. Navigating some pupils to the correct page, or even getting them to open the book, can sometimes be a struggle. Foolishly, on one occasion, I shared my frustrations with one uncooperative group in Year 10 with my top set in Year 11. From that point on, whenever we were jumping between bits of their exam texts, as soon as I'd told them which page to turn to, one of the class would very politely ask, 'What page, sir?' If I didn't immediately twig that this was a wind-up, there would be a short pause and someone else would pipe up, 'Sorry, sir, what page was that?' and then perhaps someone else until the penny dropped to loud cheers.

However, once you get started, reading is one of the safer

ways of spending the lesson. Pupils tend to dislike long passages of wordy description and can become restless, but generally class reading keeps the lid on things. The quality of the experience obviously depends on the book you're reading, and some are almost impossible to enliven. *The Old Man and the Sea* fell into this category during its unwelcome spell as a GCSE exam text, and could only be digested in short bursts. One class attempted to lighten the mood by exploiting its Hispanic setting, and read the whole thing in the voice of Manuel from *Fawlty Towers*. The only related activity which vaguely engaged the class was a mass arm-wrestle – a re-creation of the old man's marathon with the Negro from Cienfuegos.

More confident readers tend to be the hardest on their classmates who misread a word or get into a muddle, and are always ready to pounce with a chorus of derision. One unfortunate boy in Year 11 read *bible* with a short *i* – as in Officer Dibble from *Top Cat* – much to the delight of the rest of the class.

When pupils are invited to use the school library for reading or doing their homework, they nearly all make for the computers. In one previous school I used to supervise the Year 7 and 8 library during the lunch break – part of the big push to promote reading – but ended up watching pupils playing a computer game which seemed to involve manipulating stick men into various odd shapes. I don't recall seeing anyone read a book. This might have been because nearly all of the books had been removed, and replaced by an e-library where popular fiction and non-fiction titles were available on the computers. Younger pupils also have to take part in the *Accelerated Reader* programme – another expensive computer package popular with Senior Managers and Progress Leaders because it gives pupils a diagnostic assessment, a reading age (colour coded) and then lots of follow-up data – more 'evidence'.

Another way for schools to tell the outside world that it celebrates reading is via the new *I am currently reading* tag which is attached to staff emails. This represented a potentially embarrassing issue for one former colleague – a previously reading-averse Art and Design teacher who had become an avid fan of the *Fifty Shades of Grey* school of soft porn. Reluctant to share these racy titles with her colleagues she approached the English Department for some suggestions of more respectable literary titles. Over the course of the academic year, according to her *I am currently reading* tag, she read her way through *One Hundred Years of Solitude* by Gabriel Garcia Marquez, Marcel Proust's *Remembrance of Things Past, Ulysses* by James Joyce, *Bleak House* by Charles Dickens and *The Trial* by Franz Kafka.

My experience of teacher **recruitment** – of filling vacant English teaching positions – is that you generally interview from a field of two candidates, one of whom turns out to be pretty decent and gets the job. Not necessarily *'talented, energetic and visionary'* or *'excited about helping to create every aspect of the school'*, as I saw stipulated in one recent job advert, but decent teachers. Perhaps schools are setting the bar too high when they say that *'It is expected that you will be an outstanding practitioner'*. One London academy, also finely attuned to the hyper-inflationary levels of enthusiasm currently becoming the orthodoxy in secondary teaching, (but also with a suspiciously high number of vacancies) boasts of everything being *'underpinned by our six pillars'*. As there are serious teacher shortages in some areas of the country and in some subjects, instead of this rather confusing offer of *'six pillars'*, why not mention the job security, long holidays and excellent pension scheme.

PE and History are the only subjects where there isn't

a shortage of teachers. Physics teachers, on the other hand, and Science teachers generally, are like gold dust. Unlike their colleagues who teach subjects like English, or History, or RE, they have other options of employment, in areas like industry and research. This may have something to do with the absence of marking in many pupils' Science books. One former colleague – a Physics teacher – routinely threatened to leave whenever he was taken to task for not marking the students' work. The new school year invariably starts with the Head Teacher introducing another new clutch of Science and also Maths teachers, and schools sometimes have to schedule science lessons in slots after school so that they can be taught by specialist Science teachers.

Recruitment videos steer clear of anything so prosaic as holidays and pensions. The most recent government video poses the question *'Why did you choose to teach?'* to a young languages teacher. The answer comes in in the form of four or five snapshots of successful lessons – inevitably this includes Science teachers with a water rocket and fireworks – leading to the simple conclusion, *'And that is why I chose to teach'*. They never feature experienced teachers – hoary old timers with no interest in what they're wearing. Perhaps they have a point; experienced teachers, who haven't managed to manoeuvre their way out of the classroom, might not be great role models for other human beings – tired, grumpy, cynical, etc.

In the absence of attractive financial rewards something else is required to recruit graduates to a career in teaching. In a recent Teach First video this includes the promise of being one of the *'ones who open minds and open eyes'* and who *'finds that spirit, that genius, that spark'*. You must also *'love what you do'* and how you make your pupils *'feel – each and every one of them'*.

There is also a strongly political angle to the approach of Teach First to teacher recruitment. Their website is headed with blunt statements like *'Education in the UK isn't fair'* and *'Children from the poorest backgrounds aren't achieving their ambitions'*. Their video, which features David, a *Teach First* teacher in Walthamstow, also challenges the notion of futures being *'decided...just because of where their parents were born or how much their parents earned'*.

But alongside this appeal to the heart and social conscience is another, rather sneakier message – *'We do more than just teach'*. David is quietly enjoying a cup of coffee in a trendy café – not the sort of thing you can usually ever manage to do during the school day. The teacher recruitment advert on display at my local train station features four young teachers in business suits in the quiet safety of a meeting room, possibly *sharing good practice* or perhaps having a *conversation* about pupil progress. And the key message from the government recruitment video is all about *'swift career progression'*. *'Everyone just thinks I stand at the front of the class all day – that's all I do all day...'* says Mike, a *Subject Route Leader*. David says something similar in the Teach First video – *'Teachers; we do more than just teach.'* What do they mean *'just'*? Is there something wrong with just teaching? Is there something beyond launching rockets and fireworks they're not telling new recruits in the propaganda? According to DfE figures, the answer of a lot of new teachers is, probably, 'yes'. Nearly a third of new teachers who joined in 2010 went on to leave teaching within five years. And a survey from 2015 by the NUT and You Gov found that over half of all teachers interviewed were thinking of leaving within the next two years, citing the main reasons as *'volume of work'* and the need for a *'better work / life balance'*.

Teaching isn't a bad job at all, although – shock horror –

many teachers don't like their job. It has more variables which affect your day-to-day happiness and wellbeing than most jobs, but it can be enjoyable and very rewarding. It's very rarely boring, it's sociable and you generally work alongside pleasant colleagues in a mutually supportive atmosphere. But nobody can pretend it's an easy ride, or particularly well paid, or that you actually get to swan around like a prophet or visionary with a flock of inspired student admirers in tow. It's just not like that. If it were there wouldn't be a problem with teacher recruitment.

School **reports** used to be written in the staff room in a communal, even convivial, atmosphere - that was until someone made an error sufficiently bad that it required Tip-ex, photocopying, and then re-writing to fix it. Three lines was the absolute maximum you could write in each subject box and it was possible to write a class set of reports in one free period. Report time has always been most challenging for teachers of subjects like PE, RE or Citizenship – teachers who see lots of different classes, often from one year group, but teach them so infrequently that it's hard to remember all the pupils' names or have much to say about their progress. Neither helps when it comes to writing reports, especially now that we have a thousand characters to play with. Computerised reports don't offer teachers the sanctuary provided in the past by bland all-purpose phrases like *Satisfactory* or *Could do better*. One solution is to cut and paste or use statement banks, but sometimes the pupil who emerges from the report is unrecognisable to their parents, and virtually identical to the rest of their class.

Websites like *reportbankcomment.co* promise that you can '*Write your school reports in minutes not hours*'. Workload has always been the hot issue for teachers when it comes to writing reports. On my father's secondary school reports from the 1950s, his teachers had only one line available in which they could write their comment, but in fact only about a third of them wrote anything at all. 1955 (his fourth year or Year 10) was an especially barren year with just three comments – two entries of *Satisfactory* and one *Works Well*. In general the teachers seemed much harder to please. My father didn't manage a single A grade in English or English Literature, though later went on to have a successful academic career, a professorship, and more than a dozen books to his name. His Music teacher seems to have specialised in lukewarm feedback – *Fair only* and *Fairly good*. *Satisfactory* hadn't yet become second rate in the 1950s and was sometimes given a gloss with *Very satisfactory*. Steadiness was another prized asset – although the phrase *a very steady worker* has echoes of George describing Lennie to the boss at the start of *Of Mice and Men*. My mother, on the other hand, was *'not always steady'* according to her Geography teacher.

Steadiness and being damned with faint praise was also a feature of my secondary school reports at the end of the 1970s / early 1980s. My Physics teacher commended (?) me on *'steady uninspired progress'*. The more peripheral subjects in the curriculum clearly felt under no pressure to provide detailed feedback. From Summer Term Report in 1979: Music B / 3 *Good*; Metal Work B / 5 *Made progress*; and my Woodwork teacher, who probably didn't know who I was, was even less willing to commit himself – *Worked fairly well*.

Mr Hooker, the fearsome PE teacher who took us for Maths, began the year with faint praise (*'His exam result indicates that he's not the idiot he tries to be in class'*), but by the end of year report in the Summer Term the gloves were well and truly off: *'His attitude is appalling. Takes delight in playing the fool. In dire need of a good shake-up.'*

Fast forward to the present where teachers are provided with positive phrases to employ when praising their pupils. A laminated sheet entitled '*47 ways to praise each other in a Thinking Classroom*' appeared in my classroom last year, glued to the teacher's desk. Two smiley faces and a long list of phrases which included *Cool Thinking, Special Thought, Good Mistake, You're An Innovator, Cracking Comparison* and *You Are A Walking Mind Map*. Some of them seemed to have been imported from Enid Blyton and *Malory Towers* (*Terrific Creation, Excellent Brainwaves* and *Top Neurones*) and some were just plain odd – *That Is Wise, You Are Sharp*, or simply *Brainy* – though not as odd as I'd have sounded if I'd actually used any of them.

In order to cajole and control students, schools seem to be resorting, increasingly, to this sort of infantile language. What might previously have been report cards or conduct cards are rebranded as *Star Cards* or *Bingo Cards*, to be signed by members of staff if pupils have demonstrated confidence, respect, resilience or community spirit. Why would even a Year 7 pupil – an eleven or twelve year old, who might well go home and spend several hours playing on their Xbox or PS3 – work harder or behave more considerately because they are carrying a Bingo Card? It's also no coincidence that **resilience** is so high on the agenda in both primary and secondary schools. Head Teachers presumably know what pupils have to submit to if they're to achieve their Target Grades and make the school happy, but appealing to their resilience sounds like it's doing them a favour whilst hopefully delivering another marginal gain for the school's progress measure. Resilience doesn't, however, seem to include learning to tell the time. Reports ahead of this year's public exams in the summer reveal that some schools are planning to replace traditional clocks with digital ones to assist students' time keeping in the exam room.

Successive Thursdays in the second half of August are traditionally **results day** for A level students and then for pupils in Year 11 who have taken their GCSEs.

A level results come out first and will usually be accompanied by a discussion on Radio 4's *Today Programme* – initiated by a right wing think tank or *The Daily Mail* – along the lines of A Levels, previously the educational *gold standard*, being devalued by grade inflation. This isn't something I've noticed with my A Level English Literature students in recent years, but in one respect they may have a point. It's now not uncommon for good, but not outstanding students, to receive unconditional offers from universities. Presumably it's enough for the university that they appear motivated and able to pay the tuition fees. Why risk part of their income on something as unpredictable as exam results. But whether these students will then give it their all and hoist schools and departments up into the *red* (hot) zone on the *ALPS'* thermometer (*Active Learning Practices for Schools*), remains to be seen. In previous years, even when I thought pupils had all done as well or better than I had dared hope, *ALPS* had us more than halfway down the thermometer – nowhere near the *red* zone, and barely in the *black*, but hovering just above the cold *blue* at the base.

Last year's GCSE results day was reported on the BBC as the *'Govian chicken coming home to roost'*. Radio 4 featured a report in which their correspondent visited a hairdressing salon to interview the owner about the new grades for GCSE Maths and English. As the producer probably anticipated, the owner of the salon assumed that a grade 1 is the top mark rather than the equivalent of the old U grade (ungraded). There was also some discussion about whether a pass is a grade 4 or a grade 5.

The official line from the DfE is that a grade 4 is a *Standard Pass* and a grade 5 is a *Good Pass*, for now anyway.

Miraculously the government managed to simultaneously trumpet the introduction of tougher exams and still end up with improved results – all from pupils and teachers of very similar ability and work ethic to the ones who took the exam, or taught, the year before. Hard not to smell a rat when pupils suddenly start achieving the top grades again. Having averaged a miserly one A* in English for the last few years, or sometimes achieved none at all, last year we had ten grades of 8 and above (the new A*) in English Language and eleven in English Literature. Far from being allowed to suffer, the guinea pigs were given fresh hay and a new bowl of water. The safety net of having the equivalent of two C (pass) grades – grade 4 and 5 – also helped.

The new top grade – grade 9 – has a certain novelty value but doesn't have quite the same ring to it as an A*, or even an A**, and *straight As* sounds much better than *straight 9s*. Top achievers who managed 9s in Maths, English Language and English Literature, perversely ended up with the number for the emergency services. And why make the top grade a 9 instead of the more obviously attractive 10? Is it to leave the government wriggle room – extra capacity for even greater stretch and challenge – so that they can add the 10 later on, in the run-up to a general election, to crown the improvements in results under their policies.

A lot of the media discussion last year on GCSE results' day focused on the new, more demanding Maths GCSE – referred to as the *'big fat exam'*. Instead of setting exam papers for different tiers or levels of ability, there's now just one exam paper, which contains some content which a lot of pupils won't have a clue how to tackle. Likewise the English Language paper with the introduction of the specialist *structure* question and the insistence on all pupils sitting exam papers on Shakespeare and a nineteenth century novel. Schools can't protect students who might be floundering hopelessly in the face of texts they can't access because of the way GCSE performance is measured. Currently the points for English Language or English Literature count as two GCSEs, regardless of how the pupil does in the other component – Language or Literature. But it only counts double if the student has been entered for both. When this statistical special offer / anomaly was first introduced it led to some schools reportedly entering low ability English students for English Literature, who they knew hadn't a chance of passing it. It was enough to enter the exam room, put your name on the paper, and then do nothing; if you could scrape through your English Language it would still count as two GCSEs.

Not that pupils who struggle with English are being done any favours in terms of getting through the traditionally more functional English Language GCSE. *Coursework* (previously worth 20%) has gone, and so too *Speaking and Listening* (also worth 20%), which was a part of the course where pupils who had difficulty with their writing could still excel – as in later life. *Speaking and Listening* hasn't completely disappeared – it's now called *Spoken Language*, and pupils still have to do it, but it contributes no marks to their GCSE.

S

Summer Term

Study Leave

Snow Days

Shakespeare

When I went to the interview at my first school, at some point towards the end of the **Summer Term**, there was only Year 9 left at the Upper School, creating a misleading impression of cloistral hush. Year 11 and 13 students doing public exams had been released on *Study Leave* at the start of May, and Work Experience had accounted for Year 10. Another bonus for teachers who were assigned to invigilate the school exams at the Lower School for Years 7 and 8 was the 'pair system', which allowed them to organise a one day on / one day off arrangement during exam week with their other half, and days out at Wimbledon or the Test Match.

Sadly both *Study Leave* and *Work Experience* have become a thing of the past in many schools because they get in the way of pupils' *learning*. Students are often expected to continue attending lessons even when the final exams have started and the teachers have said all they have to say and exhausted every possible avenue of support. On hearing this year that study leave was being scrapped even for the sixth form, one of my old colleagues – a heroic stalwart and wonderful teacher – texted me with Boxer's refrain from *Animal Farm*: '*I will work harder*'.

Another unwelcome development is that some schools launch their Year 9 students straight into their GCSE courses as soon as they've done their end of year exams. No sooner have you said goodbye to your Year 11 GCSE classes and begun looking forward to gently winding down towards the summer holiday, than you have to start up all over again with Year 9.

One traditional aspect of the Summer Term Senior Managers can't change is the heat. It's invariably hottest to coincide with the school exam week, which is tough on students who have to sweat it out in baking classrooms whilst working flat out. Last year, to accompany the stupefying effects of the heat – temperatures reached 34 degrees during exam week – the chief topic of conversation in the staffroom was ITV2's *Love Island*. There are usually reminders, as the end of the Summer Term approaches, that standards have to be maintained, especially uniform. It's not uncommon for pupils to arrive for the lesson after lunch so hot and sweaty and fractious from running around in the playground, that it's impossible to interest them in any work. Last summer, when I was attempting to teach *Pride and Prejudice* – a novel in which the characters' idea of exercise is a '*turn around the room*' – the first ten minutes of several lessons was spent remonstrating with boys who had removed their shirts and socks. To be fair to students they don't get to work in air-conditioned offices with cold water dispensers. The projectors for the whiteboards often overheat and malfunction on hot days in the summer, so why shouldn't they when there are thirty of them crowded together in a small classroom.

The official line at this time of year is that *learning* goes on as normal – only not for the pupils away on a French trip or Music trip, or who are out of lessons doing marathon Art exams, or helping the PE Department with inter-house competitions.

There are also sometimes reminders not to succumb to showing films, although English teachers seem to do that all year round.

One response to the inevitable end of term slacking-off is the *Activities Week*. The idea is to minimise disruption by organising all trips during one week towards the end of the school year. And for those pupils not going anywhere, departments suspend the normal curriculum and organise fun activities. Easier said than done, and harder for some subjects than others. At my first school the RE department refused to take up the challenge and, instead, organised a screening of *Schindler's List* in the sports hall. To enable the students to see the relatively small TV screen the lights had to be switched off, plunging the remnants of Year 9 and the small band of staff into complete darkness. Without even any chink of natural light the pupils could muck about with impunity under the cover of total darkness for the duration (nearly three hours) of the film. Staff emerged at the end traumatised and blinking into the glare of the daylight outside.

At the very end of the Summer Term a delicious listlessness takes over and softens the hard edges, and pupils who have previously been such hard work seem like lambs in the last lesson of the year. The behaviour tends to be better and you part from most classes at the end of the last lesson like firm friends – 'See yer sir…have a good summer.'

Less inevitable than your shirt sticking to you in the Summer Term, are **snow days**, but when they do come they can be a godsend. In the dark days of January and February teachers and pupil follow the weather forecast with keen interest as soon as there is a mention of snow. Sadly the severity of the weather isn't the only issue now. Getting in the way of a day off is the zeal of new Heads, determined to keep their school open at all costs. *Learning* must go on and must be seen to go on. But there's also health and safety issues for schools to think about, so pupils face a double blow – school's still on but you aren't allowed outside to throw snowballs. Faced with the grim news that his school wasn't shutting this week because of the snow, my son wailed, 'If you're not allowed outside what's the point of even going to school?' His disappointment was understandable – the 'beast from the east' had closed another local school but his was soldiering on.

It wasn't always like this. I once arrived at school to find the playground bathed in warm sunshine with what had been a few flakes of snow melting into puddles. It wasn't even necessary to wear a coat, but strangely what staff and pupils there were had gathered in the hall – the school was closing for the day because some teachers had rung to say they couldn't get in.

Post-austerity there seems to be a more steely attitude, and going the extra mile, regardless of the inconvenience to staff and students, has become the norm.

Schools, and specifically English teachers, are required to be enthusiastic about **Shakespeare** and are taxed with organising ways to celebrate Shakespeare's birthday, in addition to *World Book Day* and *National Poetry Day*. Pupils tend to have a grudging respect for Shakespeare and seem to recognise instinctively that they are partaking in a non-negotiable rite of passage – plus there's some satisfaction at doing something which is supposed to be difficult, and about which they can groan to their younger siblings who do easier stuff in the lower years or at primary school. This was the spirit in which I approached *Macbeth* in 1982 when I was in the fourth year (Year 10). By then the Roman Polanski film version was already more than ten years old and showing its age. Our English teachers arranged a trip to the cinema to see a special screening of the film for local schools. When we got back to school we were subjected to a furious post-mortem about our behaviour, conducted by our Year Head, who also happened to be our English teacher. The first sighting of the three witches at the start of the film had been greeted with an outburst of 'That's your mum', and at the end, when Macbeth's decapitated head is waved around on the end of a pike staff, somebody from our group shouted out, 'He was game for a laugh', a reference to a popular Saturday night light entertainment show.

Pupils today are still using the Polanski film (1971) in their English lessons, and giggling when *'Playboy Productions'* appears in the opening credits, and at the cheap special effects for Macbeth's *'dagger of the mind'*, at the naked witches in Act Four Scene One (still somebody's 'mum'), and at the stiff finale – the showdown between Macbeth and Macduff.

The fight scene at the end is a particular challenge for school productions, lacking any special effects or expertise in stage fighting. During one school production, as Macbeth and Macduff slowly brought their wooden swords together, the audience, rather insensitively, began to laugh. Sensing that the scene required a bit more intensity the two schoolboy actors attacked each other inexpertly with greater gusto – resulting in Macduff suffering a nasty gash to his forehead and real blood dripping all over the floor.

Hopes of deliverance from the Polanski film was offered by the arrival of a new film version – the Michael Fassbender *Macbeth* in 2015 – but turned sour as it dawned on English teachers that the new film was virtually unusable in the classroom. There are no good fights and the actors mumble incomprehensively in thick Scottish accents, prompting students to ask for the old film instead.

Othello tends to go down better. It's a better play and there's a fantastic film version with Laurence Fishburne and Kenneth Branagh. It also combines two of GCSE and A Level students' favourite subjects – sex and racial stereotyping. Iago's line about Othello and Desdemona – *an old black ram is tupping your white ewe* – quickly becomes the much quoted answer to every question. Pupils are genuinely moved by the events at the end of the film, which are always watched in hushed silence, and then, to cover their embarrassment at their emotional reaction, someone will say 'Good film that, sir', and normal conversation resumes.

Sonnet 130 (*'My mistress' eyes are nothing like the sun'*) is based on another favourite activity of some school children – insulting each other's physical appearance – and can be put to work for the nobler end of re-creating sonnet form. Originally my *starter* activity for this involved giving pupils mini whiteboards on which to write their nature-based romantic similes, but this was usually hijacked by them drawing large cocks or rude pictures of each other, so they now write them in their exercise books instead.

T

Teachers

Timetable

Teachings Assistants (TAs)

Teacher's Pet

Teachers become teachers for all sorts of reasons. Amongst my contemporaries at university at the end of the 1980s, teaching was widely regarded as a bit of a last resort. (*'I have been in the scholastic profession long enough to know that nobody enters it unless he has some very good reason which he is anxious to conceal...'* Dr Fagan, the headmaster in Evelyn Waugh's novel *Decline And Fall*.) At my first PGCE interview I was surprised to be asked why I wanted to become a teacher. I hadn't really thought about that, and had to admit that actually I didn't really want to be a teacher, but that I needed 'something lined up for next year'. Wisely the course tutor terminated the interview after about two minutes and I found myself back out on the street scratching my head. Fortunately I had a second interview somewhere else, and put on a suit and tie and tried to say the right things.

Part of the attraction of teaching was that you could escape the harsher realities of the commercial world and stay in a world you already knew – one with job security, much nicer bosses, and longer holidays. As long as you were reasonably polite you could also say what you wanted to say without fear of reprisals. In my first teaching post my Head of Department stood up at one staff meeting and sang the Marseilles in defiance at a Senior Management initiative. And one of the PE teachers managed to nearly decapitate the minibus on the way back from a school fixture, but simply parked the bus in its usual place and went home without mentioning it to anybody. But nothing happened to him as a result of this. There were free lunches and there was a bit of room for manoeuvre.

Teachers were and are an eclectic mix of characters because they come with very different areas of interest and expertise. This is often not the *children* but their chosen subject. Many teachers are a Maths or Geography or Music teacher first, and a teacher – or *learning mentor* as it has started to be called – second. Teaching your subject is a full-time job, but is currently being made much harder by having to satisfy the *Teaching and Learning* (or *Learning and Teaching*) agenda. It's like being a professional footballer, who has to do his or her particular job on the pitch, but simultaneously is also asked to commentate on the match (*self-evaluation*) and provide analysis and match statistics. The new orthodoxy envisages teachers having conversations in their free periods about *raising achievement* and *sharing good practice*, but the reality of teaching lesson after lesson to classes of between twenty-to-thirty teenagers is that you want to put your feet up and think about something else. And when it's gone badly most teachers would rather go home, go for a drink, or crawl up into a ball, than *reflect on their practice.*

The upside of not earning as much as friends and contemporaries in the commercial world was that you didn't have to swallow all of the corporate hot air that goes with high level meetings and business launches. But now you do – in spades: *Aspiration Days, SMART Targets, Departmental Champions* for this, *Ambassadors* for that, *Leadership for Learning, Assessment for Learning, Assessment of Learning, Teaching and Learning, Learning and Teaching*. None of this helps you teach a lesson about glaciation, the respiratory system, or Bismarck's foreign policy. That hasn't changed but the endless talk about *learning* is new and is a real turn-off for most teachers and their pupils. Students don't magically improve because the pupil next to them has marked their work in green pen, or because they have *TRIP* (Time for Reflection and Improvement) or *DIRT* (Dedicated Improvement Reflection Time). Quiet reflection might be appropriate with a class who have just read of watched the end of a Shakespeare tragedy or been discussing the holocaust in a History lesson, but is it really necessary after pupils have just learnt a new element of algebra or just been shown how to use top spin in a table tennis lesson. But if you want to get on in teaching today it's best to embrace the language of *Teaching and Learning*. One former colleague made himself unpopular with some staff by declaring that he was 'passionate about plenaries' (the bit at the end of the lesson) during a staff meeting. Teachers also arrive from some of the more zealous academies with tales of having to embed each slide of their power point lesson plan with the school's crest and motto. And instead of just giving out the notices at the morning briefing, some schools are beginning the day with a *sharing good practice* slot.

I recall a Deputy Head expressing reservations about the school's involvement with *IIP* (*Investors in People*) – one of the first pointless corporate initiatives that Head Teachers signed up for in the 1990s in the hope of getting some more money. He wondered if highly educated and independent minded members of the teaching staff would play along with the external auditor, who had to visit the school to interview them. Having witnessed the robust exchanges of views at staff meetings he had a point. But that has also gone to be replaced by carefully managed celebration and displays of enthusiasm. I can't recall the last time anyone challenged anything openly in a staff meeting; instead we are given post-it notes on which to write down positives and negatives (although that word probably isn't used). It's all carefully controlled with lots of talk of 'rolling things out' and 'moving things forward'. The majority of teachers remain stonily silent throughout.

Senior Managers either genuinely like this sort of empty political language or they use it because they think it's the way to get on. Their excitement in relation to teaching – a difficult and very demanding job, often done in far from ideal conditions for modest financial rewards – is only possible because they have a far lighter **timetable**, sometimes consisting of two or three lessons over an entire week, or in the case of Head Teachers, none at all. Increasingly their attitude seems to be, in the words of Michael Jordan, someone they're fond of quoting, *just you do it*, whilst they get on with the important business of collecting evidence and sending emails, and generally finding more for classroom teachers to do. Heads and Deputy Heads have never taught many lessons but used to sensibly refrain from public shows of excitement. Head Teachers who do continue to teach the odd lesson definitely enjoy greater respect from their staff.

The **timetable** is always a potentially sticky operation for the member of the Senior Management in charge, and generally the policy is to reveal nasty surprises as late in the school year as possible. Staff often only get their final timetable for the next academic year on the last day of the Summer Term, which avoids, or at least postpones, unedifying conversations in the staff room about which colleagues 'have got more free periods than me'. It also means that teachers are generally too busy looking forward to the summer holiday to make any fuss about the idyllically empty timetables of their bosses on Senior Management. One of the other things teachers check is who they've got last period on Friday afternoon – ideally no one, and it's a free period.

TAs or **Teaching Assistants** are a bit of a mixed blessing. They are obviously there to help you but are usually assigned to your class because it contains pupils in dire need of extra support. Traditionally TAs tend to be women between middle and retirement age, skilled in being unassuming and quietly supportive. One exception was a TA who the pupils christened the Queen Mum for her haughty demeanour. She liked to rearrange the furniture whilst you were trying to talk to the class and picked fights with the pupils she was supposed to be supporting. Another TA infuriated one of my colleagues by putting up her hand to answer the questions being put to the class.

Secretly I imagine that a lot of secondary school teachers would really rather not have Teaching Assistants on hand to witness the various rows and sticky moments which take place in the classroom. There's nothing worse than sliding into the abyss of a chaotic lesson and having another adult in the room to witness your failure.

On the plus side TAs are more likely to bring cake and biscuits to the staff room – that is unless they are one of the new breed of young TAs, who are just doing it to get on a PGCSE course for the following year.

The **teacher's pet** in my secondary school belonged to our

Biology teacher. She was a very well behaved Labrador that sat impassively through Biology lessons, even when we were squirting water at each other with pipettes. In fact there wasn't much of this sort of behaviour; the dog seemed to have a significant calming influence on the class, if not her owner (our Biology teacher), who behaved as if each class was a monstrous intrusion on the quiet domestic harmony she enjoyed with the dog. She certainly had no truck with *personalised learning* for any of us and particularly resented us asking questions. Her manner was a far cry from current best practice – making a point of asking each pupil a question and then thanking them effusively whatever the response.

It's hard for teachers not to practise a certain amount of institutionalised favouritism, especially if they want the lesson to go smoothly. Why would a PE teacher, who has just taught the class techniques for close ball control, then ask a student with two left feet to demonstrate the activity dribbling round cones. Class discussion and involvement is obviously healthy but only if the majority of the responses are in some way helpful and to the point. When there are inspectors or SLT observers in the room it's hard not to turn to the pupils who you can rely on to say something sensible.

When I was in the second year (Year 8) our Woodwork teacher came in one day looking very pleased with himself and announced that he had just purchased a 'new bit of kit' – some sort of powerful mechanical saw. While he went and got some wood for the demonstration we were to select a volunteer to try it out. The class immediately and unanimously voted for the worst carpenter in the class, who happened to be me. Mr Brown wasn't having any of it – 'Don't be silly. A serious suggestion please!' – and promptly selected a multi-talented boy called Perkins as his guinea pig.

But I suppose I am no better when I give the main reading parts in a play to the pupils who can read fluently and can tell the difference between the characters' lines and the stage directions.

U

Ungraded

Uniform

The old O Level or GCSE **U grade** – short for **ungraded** – at least did what it said on the tin. Its equivalent from the new number grades is a grade 1. Quick thinking pupils, who have achieved disastrous grades, might, in some cases, be able to take advantage of the link between *one* and coming first - the Premier League and Premier Inn, etc – and claim they actually did really well.

There was nowhere to hide with a U grade. Unfortunately, my secondary school used a different exam board for French O Level – my weakest subject. Had we done the Cambridge Board, which we used for every other subject, my U grade in French might have been lost amongst the other grades on my certificate. But arriving as it did by post, separately, it made more of an impression on my parents, who were distinctly unimpressed. Not that it came as a great surprise, to me or, I imagine, to them. I had been careful to manage their expectations. In the oral exam, whilst one of us was speaking (or attempting to speak) to the external examiners, another boy would be waiting at the other end of the room, looking over some questions. This ensured that any particularly clueless answer or memorable mispronunciation was then relayed by the waiting boy to the outside world. As a result, I, and the rest of my class, knew it hadn't gone terribly well. And the listening exam, which we referred to dismissively as 'multiple guess', was always in the lap of the gods, who, as it turned out, were not smiling on me or many of my classmates that year. Modern Foreign Languages were not exactly the school's strong suit. The strongest (?) linguists within the three classes of *selected* boys were grouped into one class in Year 9 and were given the opportunity to also study German. In my year the elite German class of thirty managed three O Level passes (grades of C and above), a D grade, three Es and 23 U grades.

This sort of glaring failure doesn't fit in with today's aspirational culture. Perhaps the relaxed attitude we had to our school **uniform** was a manifestation of a deeper malaise. The badges proclaiming allegiance to rock, mod or ska music, which were worn openly and without fear of punishment on the lapels of blazers, might have been the underlying cause for our underachievement in French and German. And what must wearing our ties deliberately and subversively short and fat have done to our attitude to *learning*?

It goes without saying that badge wearing is only permitted now if it's a badge for some school role or distinction – Junior Prefect, School Council Rep, Form Captain, etc.

The DfE '*strongly encourages schools to have a uniform because it can play a valuable role in contributing to the ethos of a school*'. I am not sure how beyond the obvious sort of linkage between neat appearance and neat exercise books, if indeed that exists. Perhaps the next step should be a home / school contract committing teenagers to keeping their bedrooms tidy. It's not surprising that uniforms are enjoying such prominence in secondary schools under the Tories. Conservatives love a uniform or a dress code – the armed forces, golf clubs, the

Church of England, the Masons, the MCC – and Michael Gove was no exception in his time as Education Secretary. His white paper at the end of 2010 called for a return to *'traditional blazer-and-tie uniforms'*. According to *The Independent* all three hundred and forty seven academies enforce a strict dress code. Also mentioned in this article is an academy in Peckham, whose sponsors considered introducing a cravat into their school uniform.

One theory for why more than 96% of secondary schools in Britain insist on school uniform is that it has been a reaction to the banning of corporal punishment in 1987. As well as trying rather crudely to provide the appearance of social mobility and aspiration, school uniform is seen as a control mechanism for schools short of fire power. Alternatively it is also the battleground over which most time and energy is wasted in and out of the classroom. Pupils will always find ways to subvert school uniform. Coats and hoodies, trainers, and designer sweat shirts under blazers still make it past the guards and into the classroom, and the very slow removal of them at the start of lessons is a familiar ritual for teachers wanting to start the lesson. Now the most conscientious teachers stand at the door of their classroom and refuse entry to anyone who isn't wearing the correct uniform. But whether the battle is fought in the corridor or in the classroom it's still a horrible waste of a teacher's time, energy and spirit.

This isn't, however, usually the attitude of members of Senior Management, who seem to have boundless energy for confronting this sort of thing and have taken to standing at the school gates in the morning looking for free spirits who have flouted the uniform policy. A film clip on YouTube, entitled *'Angry dad confronts head teacher over strict Margate school uniform policy'*, shows a Head Teacher and his team at the school gates, checking pupils' uniform as they enter. It appears that pupils can only enter the school if they're wearing the correct uniform. The Head compliments some of the pupils – 'Great. Thank you. Well done.' – but is unsmiling and extremely chilly to the dad whose daughter is being refused entry for wearing plain black suede shoes instead of plain black leather shoes. The dad, whilst clearly exasperated, manages not to lose his temper or become 'angry', even when the Head's response to being told that he'll take his daughter out of the school is, 'That's fine.'

Another school in Kent hit the headlines for sending girls home for wearing their skirts too short and revealing – in the words of the Head Teacher, a former police officer, for showing *'lots of thigh'*. Parents then complained to the *Gravesend Reporter* that they were the same skirts the school had told them to buy on their website. The school had previously made the national press for sending 5% of the pupil population home in one day for breaking the new school uniform rules. It isn't difficult to understand why some teenagers resisted the new rules. The only shoes permitted by the school's uniform policy are *'plain black, sturdy leather shoes with wide flat heels'*. No jewellery is permitted except for a watch with a *'plain strap'* and a *'single pair of small studs worn in the lower lobe of the ear'*. And, like an Amish community, hair *'must be worn in simple style...an unnatural striking appearance is inappropriate'*. (*'The object of education is to teach us to love beauty'* – Plato) Any parent or pupil in doubt is invited to contact the school to get advice before having their hair styled.

I once spent two weeks in a secondary school in Austria as part of a *Winter School* run by my local EFL College in England. There was no school uniform but all pupils and staff were required to swap their outdoor shoes for felt slippers when they arrived in the morning. This not only enabled everyone to pad noiselessly around the school buildings but also seemed to discourage bad behaviour. It's hard to do *attitude* or get too big for your boots when you're wearing a pair of slippers.

With the exception of the suits on Senior Management the majority of teachers aren't really role models for Gove's *'blazer-and-tie'* combination, but instead reflect the larger tendency towards dressing less formally in the workplace. Roles have been switched: teenagers used to have the freedom to forge an identity or rebel before submitting to the work suit and weekend clothes from M & S; now pupils get the work suit all the way through school, and then later have the money and freedom to experiment when they're at work. Wearing their own clothes and growing beards helped the sixth formers at my secondary school impose discipline on younger pupils when they were doing prefect duties. They seemed like adults, which can't be said of sixth formers wearing the same school uniform as every other year. Still, that's preferable to making sixth formers wear suits or what some schools call *business dress*, which is even more depressing and pointless. Just because some people pay large sums of money to wear formal outfits at independent schools, why should the rest of us follow their example? School uniform is a *'great leveller'* according to some of those who argue for keeping it. That may be true within one school but not across society as a whole. Bizarrely a vest supplied to boys at Eton costs £15 more than the blazer worn by the pupils at my last school.

V

Visual Aids

The main **visual aid** used to be the blackboard. Conscientious teachers might write up their notes for their next lesson, move the board round to hide them from view, and then go and have a cup of tea. On occasions the teacher might return to find that their work had gone up in chalk dust due to the intervention of an inconsiderate colleague or deliberate lesson wrecking by students.

I experienced a variation of this with a Year 9 class, who had been warned they were going to have a spelling test based on their homework. Knowing that I was likely to have written the correct spellings on the board, I failed to spot that they had revealed the answers before I got to the lesson. I stood at the front gravely calling out each spelling whilst they simply peered over my shoulder and copied them from the board. I had got most of the way through the thirty spellings when I discovered what was going on to howls of derision from the class.

Hardly anything about chalk boards was good. Some teachers became remarkably adept at writing and drawing in chalk but it wasn't easy. There were also always stubs of broken chalk in your jacket pocket or at the bottom of your bag. A female PGCE student, who was on my course, reached into her bag for a piece of white chalk during one particularly stressful lesson, only to fish out a tampon. Not realising her mistake she began trying to write on the board with it, from which point the lesson never recovered.

The arrival of overhead projectors and then interactive whiteboards mean that pupils have got used to everything being accompanied by visual aids, and, in some cases, appear to have dispensed with listening altogether. I once played a class of Year 10s the film version of *Of Mice and Men* in German, as a bit of a novelty and to see their reaction to a German speaking Lennie lumbering about in the barn bemoaning his bad luck after killing his puppy. I let the film run for a few minutes but there was no reaction – the class simply hadn't noticed there was anything different.

In order to try and help pupils visualise a recurrent pattern in Alan Ayckbourn's play *Absent Friends* – the way the sensitive subject of Colin's dead fiancée is kicked back and forth like a football – I stupidly gave three groups a tennis ball to recreate this dynamic / throw at each other. The Teaching Assistant supporting me took the six best behaved boys to the hall to practice their catching whilst simultaneously reading the extract, whilst I kept an eye on two groups – one in the classroom and one in the corridor outside the Duty Manager's room. When he came out to find what the disturbance was I left him in charge of rehearsing the group and returned to the classroom to oversee what was, I was beginning to realise, a doomed educational experiment. The Duty Manager lasted five minutes before herding his group back to the classroom, dryly remarking that 'Poor Carol's been dropped on her head and given a right kicking'.

In the first version of one boy's answer, Colin, the grieving fiancée, became the ball instead of Carol. So much for the power of visualisation.

Work Experience

Another argument for *'blazer-and-tie'* school uniform and business dress in the sixth form it that it is preparation for the workplace. Confusingly the government scrapped compulsory **work experience** in 2012.

This takes place or used to take place towards the end of the Summer Term in Year 10 or early in Year 11, but has become squeezed out as schools fear the effect of losing learning time on their GCSE results. It's also a logistical hassle for schools, finding every pupil a placement or, more difficult still, getting them to arrange their own placements. Some pupils embrace it and benefit but some, often whose parents *'run their own business'*, take the easy option and get to stay in bed. Most pupils return after the two week placement as more mature and reasonable human beings, but not all make it that far. One pupil, who wanted to become a chef, was fortunate to be placed in the kitchens of The Dorchester Hotel, but was back at school by lunchtime on his first day. He'd been asked to wash and cut some vegetables, a task he considered was beneath him. Unwisely he explained this to the Head Chef and was sent packing with a volley of French swear words ringing in his ears. This situation requires schools to improvise and organise alternative work experience, which usually consists of washing staff cars in the playground.

Work Experience is a valuable opportunity for some

teenagers to shed self-consciousness and improve their Neanderthal communication skills. Speaking on the telephone can be particularly daunting for pupils more used to the shorthand of texting, or Snapchat or Instagram, but it was also the case for me on my first day at *The Whitstable Times* in 1983. The editor asked me to ring up local businesses – pubs, cafes, ice cream parlours – to see what effect the exceptionally hot weather was having on trade. Just stating my name and business to a succession of bemused small business owners was difficult and embarrassing, and not made any easier by the editor and his three reporters (the entire staff) loudly taking the mick behind me.

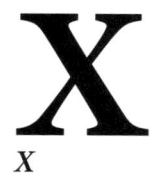

X

X is traditionally entered on the exam board mark sheets for pupils who have been absent or failed to submit any work.

One of my best friends at secondary school achieved the rare double in his A Level English of an A grade for his course work and an X in the exams, prompting the exam board to contact the school and demand an explanation. Reluctantly the school had to admit that he'd just sat through all of his exams doing nothing, as he had in all of his school and public exams (except Art) from the moment he had downed tools in the Maths mock exam in the fifth year. It was hard not to admire his stubborn independence of mind, though being an extremely talented artist and musician must have helped him stick to his guns. But neither can be relied on to pay their way and he ended up as a primary school teacher and then Head Teacher.

Year Managers

Yet

What used to be known as **Year Heads** or **Year Managers** have been rebranded in some schools as *Progress Leaders*. Instead of mainly dealing with behaviour issues their role has been re-defined in line with the progress agenda. Year Heads have tended to be drawn from subjects like PE, DT and Art – teachers who don't have so much marking or preparation to do and can afford the time to chase up pupils in detention. One way for *Progress Leaders* to be seen to be intervening and making a difference to the academic fortunes of their year group, is by placing pupils on report, and as the GCSE exams approach lots of well-behaved and hard-working students, who the data says are slightly below their inflated targets, start carrying around report cards which teachers need to fill in at the end of the lesson. Another job. Unsurprisingly some *Progress Leaders* would rather go back to collaring unruly pupils.

Yet is a word that has started to be of interest to people in schools who like talking about *learning* and *progress* – as in *'we're not there, yet'*. If a school can show it's *'moving forwards'* or *'working towards'* the promised land / *Outstanding* then all will be well when Ofsted visit.

    The Royal Society of Arts also recommends that teachers

should tell students that they haven't *yet* achieved a particular grade, rather than they've *failed* to achieve it. Along with keeping potted plants in the classroom this is one of their recommendations to encourage schools to adopt a more positive mind set and raise student morale. Teachers also have to become *'lead learners'* in order to instil the attitude that education is a continuous process.

This is all too *'woolly'* for the *Campaign for Real Education*, who connect this sort of thinking with the *'loony left'* of the *'1960s and 70s'* – *'It is trendy ideas like this that have betrayed generations of children.'*

But there's nothing wrong with softening the blow for pupils who haven't done well – particularly when there's not much prospect of them ever doing very well in a particular area. Marking doesn't have to be a scientific and entirely objective diagnosis. Sometimes the patient needs cheering up. There's no point in giving out A grades to weak students, but there's no need to always be brutally honest. Awarding a C-, which has a reassuring ring of respectability, is more likely to keep a struggling student working than a succession of E grades. (*'We school masters must temper discretion with deceit.'* – Dr Fagan, the headmaster of Llanabba School in *Decline and Fall* by Evelyn Waugh*).*

Z

Zero Tolerance

Zeal

Zombies

One of the problems of writing an *A-Z* is finding something to say when you get to Z. Sadly **Zero Tolerance** behaviour policies have come to my aid. It's hard to believe that any teacher can really enforce this in their classroom and still enjoy a healthy working relationship with their pupils. Like a football referee keeping a close eye on the shenanigans in the penalty box when a corner is about to be taken, if you really applied zero tolerance, there'd be no one left on the pitch / in the classroom. Isn't a good referee supposed to be able to talk to the players and have a bit of a laugh. Presumably schools don't really believe in zero tolerance either because behaviour policies usually involve a *Three Strike* or *Traffic Light* system, which give pupils a couple of chances to sort out their behaviour. According to the *Mail Online* a *'government expert'* went even further in 2011, recommending that a *'zero tolerance behaviour policy'* should be adopted by all schools *'for pupils AND teachers'*. Schools should use a *'checklist'* system to ensure that they run smoothly and staff should also be disciplined *'if they failed to live up to the standards they demand of their pupils'*. Like insisting that pupils walk through the corridors in silence, it all sounds so straightforward, but would that mean teachers also being required to walk everywhere without speaking. And what about taking a cup of coffee with you into the classroom? And why should anyone walk about in silence, outside of a service or moment of remembrance or a Quaker meeting house?

In their **zeal** for learning and an Ofsted Outstanding, school leaders have begun to treat teenagers like highly disciplined, grade-obsessed **zombies**, who can be appealed to via worthy slogans and controlling messages like Aim High, Work Hard and Be Kind. This isn't reserved only for teenagers. My daughter knows all of the words to a song called *The Power in Me* because she has been made to sing it so often in assembly at her primary school. Instead of starting the day with *Morning Has Broken* she and her classmates have to sing words such as '*no one can stop me learning...Create my dreams and future, and I will feel empowered from within...I've got the power...*'

She thought it was a joke when she first sang it when she was eight or nine. She's now eleven and thinks it's a complete joke, or, as my former colleague used to whisper at staff meetings, 'It's all a load of bollocks'.

The airwaves in schools are filling up with this sort of pointless and embarrassing nonsense. (Zeppelin: a large cylindrical rigid airship.) But for most of the pupils and teachers I've met this stuff is more lead balloon than Led Zeppelin. It is, as teenagers would say today, literally, a complete load of bollocks.

24908225R00083

Made in the USA
Columbia, SC
29 August 2018